WILL MEDICINE STOP THE PAIN?

Finding God's healing for depression, anxiety & other troubling emotions

WILL MEDICINE STOP THE PAIN?

Finding God's healing for depression, anxiety & other troubling emotions

ELYSE FITZPATRICK & LAURA HENDRICKSON, M.D.

MOODY PUBLISHERS

CHICAGO

IMPORTANT NOTICE:

In all matters related to taking medications or withdrawing from them,
it is absolutely essential for you to consult your physician. For suggestions
on how to do this, see appendix B at the end of this book.

© 2006 by
ELYSE FITZPATRICK AND LAURA HENDRICKSON

Cover Design: Rule 29
Cover Image: Getty, Stockbyte

Library of Congress Cataloging-in-Publication Data

Fitzpatrick, Elyse, 1950-
    Will medicine stop the pain? : Finding God's healing for depression, anxiety,
& other troubling emotions / Elyse Fitzpatrick & Laura Hendrickson.
        p. cm.
    Includes bibliographical references.
    ISBN-13: 978-0-8024-5802-5
    1. Healing—Religious aspects—Christianity. 2. Spiritual healing.
3. Depression, Mental—Religious aspects—Christianity. 4. Mental illness
—Religious aspects—Christianity. 5. Mental health—Religious aspects
—Christianity. I. Hendrickson, Laura. II. Title.

BT732.2.F58 2006
248.8'625—dc22

2006005978

ISBN: 0-8024-5802-5
ISBN-13: 978-0-8024-5802-5

1 3 5 7 9 10 8 6 4 2

Printed in the United States of America

IN LOVING MEMORY OF BILL
1950–1998

Truly, truly, I say to you, unless a grain
of wheat falls into the earth and dies,
it remains alone; but if it dies, it bears much fruit.

JOHN 12:24

IMPORTANT PUBLISHER NOTICE

This book in not intended, nor should it be interpreted, to state or imply that any particular drug, pharmaceutical company, therapy, medical diagnosis, or counseling program is wrong or harmful. All of the medications identified in this book by brand name or by generic name can play an appropriate role when expertly matched to a particular mental disease or serious emotional crisis. But do we in our depression, like King Asa in 2 Chronicles 16, run too easily and first to the medical and counseling establishments for relief in drugs when the solution may be found in the Bible and prayer? That is the challenge of *Will Medicine Stop the Pain?* If you have picked up this book because of its title, you probably have already answered the question posed by the title and are looking for more biblical and effective alternative opinions and "treatments."

CONTENTS

PART ONE:
OUR BODIES, EMOTIONS,
AND THE PROBLEM OF SUFFERING

PART TWO:
SEEKING ANSWERS WITH GOD'S HELP

APPENDICES

INDEX OF DIAGRAMS

FOREWORD

MY FRIEND ELYSE Fitzpatrick and her coauthor Laura Hendrickson have courageously and compassionately ventured into territory "where angels fear to tread"! This book is certain to evoke intense reaction from many quarters. However, it is a book that is long overdue and desperately needed.

The authors raise important questions about a way of thinking in relation to emotional pain that has become deeply engrained in our culture. Even many committed Christians have unwittingly been influenced and co-opted by widely accepted beliefs about this subject without holding those assumptions up to the scrutiny of Scripture.

This book will challenge some deeply and passionately held beliefs of sincere, well-meaning people—including many mental health and medical professionals, counselors and therapists, Christian authors, speakers, and leaders. It will challenge the choices and conclusions of many who suffer emotional pain, as well as the counsel of friends and family members who seek to help them.

So why tackle the topic? Why swim upstream against the strong, prevailing current of much of the medical and therapeutic establishment?

Because the Truth sets people free.

Because millions of people who struggle with depression, fear, anxiety, and other difficult emotions are being offered, at best, temporary relief from their pain, but are not finding lasting release from the problems underlying that pain.

Because our problems and struggles take on a whole different light when seen through the lens of the bigger, eternal plan and purposes of God.

I believe the perspective and principles set forth in this book will provide hope and help for many who have given up hope. They may be "managing" their pain, but they are not experiencing the grace of God to get to the heart issues that may have produced that pain.

Elyse and Laura's clear, biblical treatment of this subject makes this a great resource for friends, family members, pastors, and counselors who are called upon to offer insight and help to those who suffer.

I shared this manuscript with a friend before it went to press. I believe her response is representative of what many women will experience in these pages:

> *Nancy, I can hardly wait until this book is published. It was such a blessing to me in dealing with my "dysfunctional" past; I can't wait to give my sister and mother each a copy. This is one of those transformational books that must be on every woman's bookshelf. No! Forget the bookshelf; this is a book that needs to saturate every hurting woman's thoughts and heart. There are genuine, biblical answers here!*

I urge you to read this book all the way through—with a prayerful heart and an open mind. It may be one of the most important, helpful books you have read. It will likely challenge your thinking on many fronts. It will certainly give you a vision for how your suffering (and the suffering of others) can become a path to great blessing and growth and can result in the display of God's glory in this fallen world.

NANCY LEIGH DEMOSS

BILL AND
LAURA'S STORY

IT IS GOOD FOR ME THAT I WAS AFFLICTED, THAT I
MAY LEARN YOUR STATUTES.

Psalm 119:71

BILL WAS A MUCH-LOVED eldest son, and I was the next-oldest child in our family of eight. Our father was a successful professional, and our mother was an intelligent and committed full-time mom. Our parents were children of the Depression era and wanted to give everything to their children that they themselves had lacked. They provided Bill, my other brothers and sisters, and me with a prosperous and loving home.

He was a different kind of kid. Bill was very intelligent, but shy and socially awkward. We were both happy and secure young children, but when we moved into the upper grades at school we both began to experience taunting and rejection from our classmates.

Bill continued into adulthood relatively friendless and terribly lonely, never mastering the social skills required for more than superficial relationships. Years later, when I gave birth to an autistic son, more than one relative commented that it seemed that Bill had had some of the same kinds of problems, only much milder. By the time this was recognized, however, it was already too late to do anything about it.

The cancer diagnosis came in his early thirties. This devastated Bill and led to a diagnosis of depression. He was placed on medicines, and although he said that they made him feel better, in retrospect it is clear that he began a slow deterioration that finally ended with his death fifteen years later.

Although Bill beat the cancer, he never really seemed to recover emotionally from his depression. Over the years, more and more medicines and diagnoses were added. Bill was originally a slender, good-looking man, but because of the medicines, he became bloated and obese and suffered from numerous side effects.

More upsetting to those of us who loved him was the change in his personality. He had always had a quiet, light sense of humor, and he was a kind young man. But as the years advanced he became bitter, blaming our parents for his unhappiness and verbally abusing them for what he insisted were their failures to meet his needs as he was growing up. He also grew more and more self-centered. The only relationships he was able to sustain were with those who were trying to help him with his problems.

As a teenager, I had responded to rejection in a different way than Bill. I rebelled, abused drugs, and even dropped out of high school at one point. I was late when it came to settling down to build a stable adult life for myself, but ultimately I reached a high level of educational and professional achievement, became a Christian, got married, and had a son. I also became depressed in my thirties when long hours at work, marital problems, and the care of an infant overwhelmed me. Consequently, I was placed on medicines.

My personality changed quickly. I had struggled with emotional instability during my years of drug abuse, but after two years of therapy I had given up my destructive habits and seemed to have put them behind me for good. But the antidepressants suddenly made me more unstable than ever before. I was a practicing psychiatrist, but I tormented myself over my inadequacy, believing myself unfit to help anyone else because I saw myself as so disturbed.

My doctor diagnosed bipolar disorder and added more medicines. I had always been a slender woman, but at this time I gained forty pounds and my hair began to fall out. However, I felt better, and credited my diagnosis of bipolar disorder and its treatment.

I did well for a while. My son was diagnosed with autism, and I relocated with him to Los Angeles to participate in his early intervention training, and continued to work with him after he graduated from the program and we returned home. Friends and family members commented on what a patient and dedicated mother I was. I became active in my church and community and helped other mothers of autistic children.

I told my brother Bill, who still was not doing well, that I had been diagnosed with bipolar disorder, and I wondered if perhaps he had it too. He saw his doctor, was also diagnosed with bipolar disorder, and the medicines I was taking were added to his regimen. He, too, felt better and began to sense a new hope for his future.

But my improvement did not continue. I began sliding downward emotionally, and every few months, a new medicine would be added to my regimen. I felt mentally confused and continued to struggle with unstable emotions. Thoughts of suicide, which I had not had since I gave up drug abuse years before, returned with a vengeance. I was again tormented with shame over my instability and my perceived personal failures.

I hit rock bottom one horrible night when I found myself sitting on the edge of my five-year-old son's bed while he slept, a pillow in my hands, struggling with the urge to smother him and then go jump off a bridge. I had never had violent suicidal thoughts before, but these were nearly overpowering. Frightened and ashamed, I told my husband that I needed to go to the hospital. My husband called our pastor, and he agreed to meet with me immediately. What a life-changing visit that turned out to be!

My pastor told me that I did not have to live like this. He told me that Christ had come to set me free from mental agony like this, and that if I looked to Him for victory over my tormenting thoughts, He would enable me to begin thinking thoughts that led to peace instead of despair. We prayed together for God's power over my thoughts, and I felt flooded by a sense of peace. My pastor warned me that the thoughts would come back, but that I must resist by correcting those thoughts with the truths of Scripture.

I didn't go to the hospital that day. Instead, I practiced what my pastor had told me to do, and had success with this new way of thinking. My depression and suicidal thoughts left me. After a couple of weeks I decided that the medicines were confusing me and making it more difficult for me to think the truth, so I stopped taking them. In fact, it was the medicine that went off the bridge instead of me!

I began to study what God's Word has to say on the subject of unstable emotions and apply those truths more and more consistently in my life. My emotional instability was not broken in an instant, but as time went on, I became more grounded and stable. Even when I faced my own diagnosis of cancer a few years later, I took my fears to Christ and endured a grueling yearlong treatment course without becoming depressed.

I told Bill about my spiritual breakthrough. Bill, who belonged to a church that emphasized ritual over personal relationship with Christ, sought help from his pastor, who told him, "We don't do that in our church." Bill continued to struggle with his emotions. He told me that he would surely kill himself one day if he did not find a medicine regimen that would make him happy and give him a rewarding life. I told him repeatedly that he would never find happiness and a rewarding life from medicine alone; he needed a vital relationship with Jesus Christ.

The night that Bill decided he would never find the happiness he sought, he didn't tell anyone. He didn't even leave a note. He simply got into his car in a closed garage and quietly went to sleep. He was forty-eight years old.

I miss him so much! I promised myself that his death would not be in vain and committed myself to telling others of the peace and hope that I have found. This book is, in a very real sense, a fruit of his death because his loss has motivated me to tell others about how Jesus Christ can set the suffering soul free.

Today I am a biblical counselor and writer. And I am still working on the lifelong process of learning to cope with my emotions in a way that consistently honors God and serves my family, church, and the larger Christian community. I still struggle sometimes, and I fail sometimes. The unstable habits of a lifetime are not broken in a day. But I have been medication-free for twelve years, and I can testify that God's pattern for emotional peace, as taught in the Bible, has truly set me free.

Dear struggling sister, wherever you fall on the spectrum of emotional difficulties, from mild to severe, please know that this book, which I've written with fellow biblical counselor Elyse Fitzpatrick, contains answers that can help you begin your own pilgrimage from fear to faith, and from instability to peace in Christ. May He bless you as you look to Him for answers, and may this book be part of His answer to you.

A WORD OF CAUTION: If you are presently on any form of medicine intended to help stabilize your emotions, please do not stop taking it unless you are under the direct supervision of your physician and you do so at a very slow pace. Because these medicines are habit-forming, you could experience any of a number of very serious side effects, and your doctor will need to monitor these changes.

THE CRY
OF YOUR
HEART

O LORD, YOU HEAR THE DESIRE OF THE AFFLICTED;

YOU WILL STRENGTHEN THEIR HEART.

Psalm 10:17 (ESV)

Lord, please make these feelings stop! Is that the cry of your heart? If so, you are not alone. You can be encouraged by the knowledge that countless other women have learned how to have real victory over troublesome emotions. Interspersed throughout the pages of this book you will find some of their stories—all from women who have looked to God in the midst of their pain and been transformed.

It's been our experience that most of the women we counsel are struggling with their feelings. They sometimes wonder why God hasn't taken away their pain, and why He hasn't answered their prayers for help.

Perhaps your difficulties have caused you to despair of ever experiencing the abundant life that Jesus promised to believers (John 10:10). Perhaps they have even caused you to question your faith in God. But the good news is that the Bible contains specific principles that can teach us to handle our problems in a stable, God-honoring way. As we learn to apply these principles, we can begin to enjoy the abundant life that is part of our inheritance if we are children of God. (If you are not sure whether you're a Christian, you will want to read appendix A right now, on page 201.)

YOU'RE NOT ALONE

If you're a Christian, you can have confidence that you don't face your trials alone. God has promised to be with you and will help you learn and grow. When you're feeling down, it's easy to think that you are alone or that God has abandoned you. Perhaps you haven't been aware of God's presence for so long that it doesn't even seem to matter anymore. So right now, we want to remind you of His presence here with you. The Bible says, "Do not fear, for I am with you; Do not anxiously look about you, for I am your God. I will strengthen you, surely I will help you, Surely I will uphold you with my righteous right hand" (Isaiah 41:10 ESV).

Stop for a moment and reflect on God's promises to you. Read through them aloud so that you can hear the truth of His everlasting love for you: *Don't be afraid,* He's telling you. *I'm right here. You don't have to look anxiously about; I'm your God. You don't have to rely on your own strength anymore. I will strengthen and help you. And just when you feel like you're going down for the last time, I'm going to uphold you with My hand.*

So even though you may be suffering emotionally right now, and even if you are afraid to think about your troubles, remember that God is with you as you begin this journey of self-discovery. Why not take time right now to pray and ask the Lord to open your heart to seeking the solutions to your problems? Then thank Him for His presence in your life, and the comfort that knowledge brings to your heart.

As we turn now to look at what the Bible has to say about our emotions, don't forget what you've just prayed about. God is with you, and He won't leave you—no matter how you feel. *His promises are stronger than all your feelings.*

ONE MORE NOTE: If you are presently suffering with any troubling emotion, you might want to skip ahead to chapter 3, where you'll learn about God's purposes and care even in your pain. Afterward, you can come back to chapters 1 and 2, which contain a more academic discussion of emotions. These chapters are important for your understanding but might seem disconnected or difficult to you right now.

PART ONE

OUR BODIES, EMOTIONS, AND THE PROBLEM OF SUFFERING

WHAT'S WRONG WITH ME?

(꽃)

HIS DIVINE POWER HAS GRANTED TO US EVERYTHING
PERTAINING TO LIFE AND GODLINESS, THROUGH THE
TRUE KNOWLEDGE OF HIM WHO CALLED US BY HIS
OWN GLORY AND EXCELLENCE.

2 Peter 1:3

NOT LONG AGO, Julie approached me (Laura) at a conference where I was speaking to ask my advice about her depression.

"Can you tell me about how your problem began?" I asked.

"I'm not sure," she responded. "One day I just began to feel sad for no apparent reason. Over time I lost my appetite and had difficulty falling and staying asleep at night. Now I often cry for no reason. My doctor tells me that I have depression, and that I need to take medicine to cure it. Do you think that medicine would help me?"

I asked Julie about anything that might have happened shortly before the onset of her symptoms, and she told me she couldn't think of any significant changes that had occurred in her life. Then I asked her some general questions about her marriage, family, work, and faith.

Julie told me that she felt trapped in a loveless marriage. In addition, her ten-year-old son was a behavior problem in school. And her teenage daughter had been caught abusing illegal drugs. Julie was also worried she might be laid off from her job soon.

"As for my faith, I'm really struggling with why God would allow all these things to happen to me," Julie concluded.

"Wow, you have a lot of serious problems!" I exclaimed. "I think many people would be tempted to lose heart and question their faith in God if they had even a few of your problems."

"No, that's not it," Julie objected. "I mean, I do have problems, but I think I have a disease, and I'd be depressed even if I didn't have these problems. My doctor says that when your depression comes on you out of the blue like this, it is a disease, not just problems. He said that when this happens, it means I need medicine."

WHERE ARE THESE FEELINGS COMING FROM?

Many women experiencing painful emotions similar to Julie's are confused about what is happening to them and wonder what, if anything, they can do about them. Some women, after trying for years to find the right answers, have become convinced their pain is a disease and that only medicine can make them feel normal again. Well-meaning doctors may even have told them that they cannot possibly hope to improve without the help of medicine.

Other women notice that there seems to be a connection between their pain and the difficulties they are facing, and feel uneasy about taking a drug to solve what may really be an emotional problem. Yet their loved ones urge them to take medicine, reasoning that it's important for them to start feeling better as soon as possible. This does seem to make sense, doesn't it? Why wouldn't we want to take a pill if it can make our emotional pain go away?

In this chapter, we'll learn what the Bible teaches about our physical and spiritual makeup. We'll also discuss what the Bible teaches about the origin of our emotions, and how our responses to them can make our problems better or worse.

Along the way you'll be introduced to a biblical perspective of our nature as human beings created by God. This information may be new to you, and perhaps you never considered learning about God's design of the body in order to understand your emotions. But as you read on, you'll see there is a definite connection. And what you learn will give you a foundation upon which you can make better-informed decisions about your emotional pain.

INTRODUCING THE "REAL YOU"

The Biblical Perspective

Many passages in the Bible teach that we are duplex beings.[1] That is, we consist of two distinct aspects: a body or outer person, and a spirit or inner person. Your outer person is what everyone around you sees and is most aware of—it's the "you" everyone recognizes. On the other hand, your inner person, what the Bible calls the "heart," "soul," "mind," or "spirit," is the hidden side of you that thinks, feels, and makes choices.[2] This inner person is the real you that God sees and interacts with (1 Samuel 16:7; Hebrews 4:13). Your inner person is the source of the activity that can be measured in the brain, which is part of your outer person, or your physical body.

When a woman is feeling sad inside, her body reveals that sadness outwardly in her face, the tone of her voice, and her actions. We can often guess what she is thinking, feeling, or choosing on the inside because it affects what is happening on the outside. *Our speech and behavior are the body's outward expression of our inner life.* Jesus taught this truth when He said, "The good man out of the good treasure of his heart brings forth what is good . . . for his mouth speaks from that which fills his heart" (Luke 6:45).

It's obvious that our bodies can respond to the thoughts, feelings, and choices from our inner person with noticeable physical changes. For instance, our blood pressure rises and our cheeks flush when we become angry. This works the other way too. Our physical bodies can also influence our thoughts, feelings, and choices. For instance, an untreated rapid heartbeat can cause us to feel anxious, even if there is nothing to be worried about. Physical pain or illness can also produce a variety of painful or negative emotional responses.[3]

A BIBLICAL VIEW OF PEOPLE

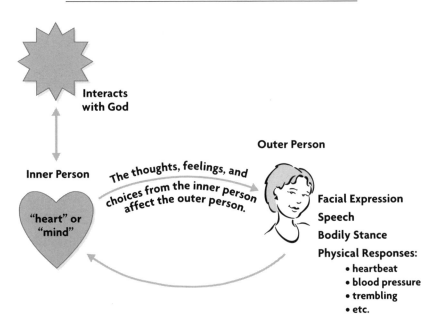

Interacts
with God

Outer Person

Inner Person

The thoughts, feelings, and choices from the inner person affect the outer person.

"heart" or
"mind"

Facial Expression

Speech

Bodily Stance

Physical Responses:
- heartbeat
- blood pressure
- trembling
- etc.

The Materialist Perspective

The Bible teaches you are made up of two distinct yet interacting parts: an outer person and an inner person. In contrast to this biblical teaching, many people today believe that we consist solely of a body. This view is called *materialism,* which is the belief that the material world (what we can sense and measure) is all that there is. A true materialist does not believe in God, the afterlife, or the inner person. A materialist would deny that the faith you hold dear is anything more than the evolved firing off of certain nerve synapses in your brain.

It seems clear we can't hold to a materialistic view and a Christian view at the same time, doesn't it? Even so, many of us who believe in the Bible are prone to think as materialists do when it comes to our health. Although we believe in an unseen and powerful inner or spiritual realm that exists beyond the physical world, we can sometimes lose sight of that inner realm when we think about how our bodies work.

We're sure you'll agree it is very important for your faith to serve as the foundation upon which you make decisions about your health. In order for that to happen, you need to understand how the materialistic view of the body contradicts the biblical teachings about the nature of humanity.

Our Beliefs Shape Our Conclusions

A materialist believes that the physical brain is the part of us that thinks, feels, and makes choices. He believes that our thoughts, feelings, and choices depend *solely* upon the balance of our brain's chemicals. A materialist would say that what we experience as consciousness is simply part of the chemical activity that takes place in the brain.

The materialist believes that our thoughts come solely from our brain's activity because scientific studies have shown a connection between our brain's functions and our thoughts, feelings, and choices. The data that the materialist is looking at is valid. The brain does change when a person is thinking, feeling, or choosing, and these changes can be measured. But the conclusions the materialist draws from this data are false because he bases these conclusions on his belief that the physical world is all there is.

Here's an example of how our beliefs shape our conclusions: If I believe that the world is flat, when I look out at the ocean (which I love to do every summer), I'll think that the horizon I see must be the edge of the world. If I believe that what I can see with my eyes is the only truth (and the earth sure *seems* flat!), I may even laugh at those who try to tell me that the earth is round.

We all interpret what we see based upon what we believe. If you believe that you consist of a body *and* an inner person, then you'll interpret problems with your emotions differently than you would if you believed that you were solely a physical body.

For the Christian, then, the interpretation of scientific information has to begin with an unchanging assumption: *God's Word is true.* Our interpretation of everything we see and hear must begin with this belief. When we look at scientific facts through the lens of Scripture, we will arrive at very different conclusions than the ones materialists reach when they look at the same facts through the lens of their assumptions.

That brings us to a key point for this book: The Bible clearly teaches that our invisible inner person (not our brain) is the source of our thoughts and intentions (Hebrews 4:12), our emotions (Romans 9:2), and our choices (Matthew 15:18). When the Bible talks about our thoughts, sometimes it calls the inner person the *mind* (Romans 8:7; 12:2). Other times Scripture talks about our thoughts originating in our *heart* (Matthew 15:19; Mark 7:21; Hebrews 4:12). The exact word used to refer to the inner person is not so important. But whatever we call it, we want to remember that our thoughts, choices, and feelings originate from the inner person, not in the physical matter of the brain.

Because this is true, the real and measurable chemical activity of our brain is simply a *reflection* of what is going on in our heart, or inner person, and not the *source* of our thoughts, feelings, and behavior. The inner person, or heart, is the source of our outer, physical words and actions. Professor of practical theology Dr. Edward Welch summarizes the interaction between the inner person and the brain in this way: "It is as if the heart always leaves its footprints on the brain."[4]

The following diagrams will help you see the differences between the biblical view and the materialist view:

THE BIBLICAL VIEW:
OUR INNER AND OUTER PERSON

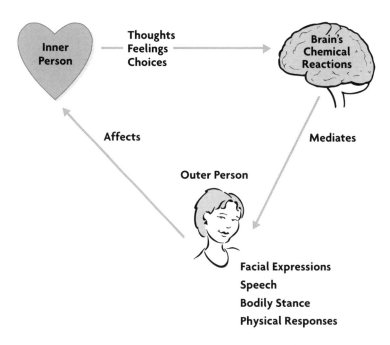

The heart or mind thinks, feels, or chooses, and this registers on the brain and results in words and actions.

THE MATERIALIST VIEW:
NO INNER PERSON

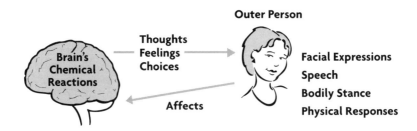

The chemical reactions in the brain create our thoughts, feelings, or choices, which in turn leads to various physical functions.

The biblical view, then, can be summed up this way:

- Christians hold to the unchanging assumption that God's Word is true.
- The Bible teaches that we consist of two parts: the physical body and the inner person.
- There is much interaction between our body and our inner person. Our body can influence our inner person, and vice versa.
- Generally speaking, the changes that occur in our brain when we take any action, or when we feel sad or anxious, originate in our inner person. These changes in the brain can be measured and studied, but the brain is not the place where thoughts or feelings originate. As we've demonstrated from the Bible, they come from the invisible inner person.[5]

IS EMOTIONAL PAIN A DISEASE?

Our friend the materialist would strongly disagree with the biblical view and would say that a healthy brain produces happy feelings, comfortable thoughts, and good behavior. He would view negative feelings, thoughts, or behavior as disease, an uncomfortable and undesirable condition due to a dysfunction in the brain.

Could there be a different reason for our emotional pain? What would you do if you began to have severe pain in the lower right side of your abdomen? Would you take pain pills to stop the pain, or would you check to see if you had appendicitis? Abdominal pain is a sign that something is wrong in your abdomen. It is not a disease in its own right. In the same way, emotional pain or distressing thoughts may be signs that something is not right with our heart, or inner person.

In the same way that our cars come equipped with warning lights to let us know when there is a problem with the engine, our gracious heavenly Father has created our bodies with the capacity to experience pain, and that pain serves as a "warning light" for our bodies. When we see a warning light on our dashboard, we get our car checked out; we don't just ignore the light or place black tape over it so we don't have to look at it. When we have physical pain, we go to a doctor to get examined; we don't just take pain pills and hope that will solve the problem. In the same way that pain medicines will not cure appendicitis but will only cover up the signs, medicine directed at our emotions may only cover up the signs that what we really have is "heart trouble."

Emotional pain is not a disease. It is a sign of a problem with our heart, just as abdominal pain is a sign of appendicitis. Remember that one of the words the Bible uses for the inner person is *heart*. In biblical terms, then, we have "heart trouble" when we are struggling with our thoughts, emotions, or desires.

Please note that this truth does not necessarily rule out the possibility that a physical problem may also be affecting our feelings, in the same way that a rapid heartbeat can produce anxiety. Remember that our inner person can affect our physical health, and our physical health can affect our inner person. But generally speaking, "problem" feelings are an indicator of a problem in our inner person.

In either case, our feelings aren't dysfunctional or sick. Our feelings are doing just what they were created by God to do. They're showing us that we have a problem. *To feel better, we need to fix the problem, not just make the pain go away.*

WHAT CAN OUR FEELINGS TELL US?

Our emotions are given to us by God in part to let us know about the condition of our inner person. He didn't give us emotions so we could let them rule our lives or even guide us in making decisions. The line often heard in sentimental movies, "Trust your feelings," is not God's advice. We should not make decisions based on how we feel. Instead, God has given us His Word to direct our thoughts and choices.

Although we should not be *led* by our emotions, we do need to *listen* to them. We should be aware of them because they can help us understand what's going on inside of us. Here's an example: If I assume that I'm loving God with all my mind but I am constantly anxious about the future, then my anxiety may be telling me something about my inner person that I wasn't aware of. Perhaps my anxiety about the future tells me I've allowed other things to become more important to me than God, such as fear of loss or the love of money.

Rather than seeking to deaden, ignore, or elevate the importance of our emotions, we should allow them to speak to us about our hearts. Because God gave us the ability to experience emotions, we want to be very cautious about ignoring what they may be telling us. We want to carefully consider whether dampening the awareness of our feelings through the use of medication (or alcohol) is the best road for us to take to better health.

Medicines or alcohol may make us feel better for a time, even if our "heart problem" is not addressed. For example, we know that morphine dulls the pain of a broken arm. It does not heal or reset the bone, and it does not fix the root cause of the pain. The same is true about medicines and emotional pain. In order to resolve such pain, we need to deal not with the symptoms, but the root causes of the pain.

Please understand we are not saying there are no physical causes for emotional pain. The brain itself can develop diseases, just as the rest of our body can. Alzheimer's disease, for example, causes physical changes in the cells of the brain, leading to their death. Disease processes in other organs can also affect the brain, causing changes in our thoughts and feelings. *But this is very different from considering bad feelings or uncomfortable thoughts, in themselves, to be brain diseases.*

In summary, then:

- God gave you emotions so you can recognize what's happening in your inner person.
- Your decisions should not be based on your emotions.
- Troubling emotions are not, in themselves, brain diseases.
- Instead of seeking to deaden our painful emotions, we need to listen to what they're telling us and respond in faith to the Lord and His Word.

WHY IS BIBLICAL PERSPECTIVE SO IMPORTANT?

Why is having a biblical understanding of our emotions so important? Because we consist of both a spirit *and* a body, and any solution to our problems that leaves out the spiritual side is only a partial solution.

What's more, the materialistic view of the brain has very serious implications for our faith. *If our thoughts and choices are determined solely by the physical activity of our brains rather than by our inner person, then when we do wrong, it must not be our fault. A disease must be to blame.*

Stop and think carefully about what we've just said. Doesn't the Bible teach us that we must believe in Christ to be saved from the penalty our sins deserve? And that we should evidence that belief through our thoughts and behavior? But if our inner person is not the source of our thoughts and choices (as the materialist believes), then we can't possibly be pronounced "guilty" of our sins. If we aren't guilty, we don't need a Savior. And if we don't need a Savior, then Christ's death was in vain. This is not what the Bible teaches.

According to the biblical view, what is the prescription for our problems? The cross of Christ.

THE BIBLICAL DIAGNOSIS

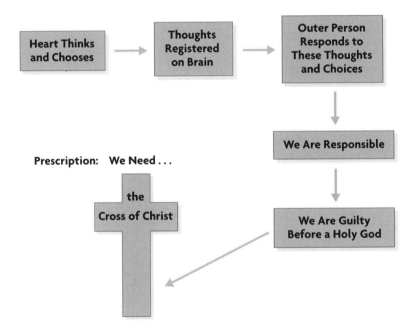

THE MATERIALIST'S DIAGNOSIS

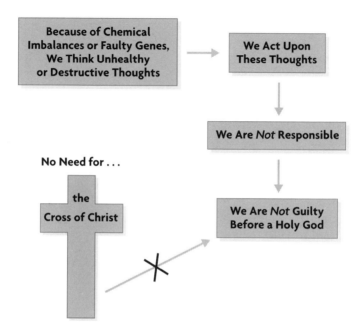

The materialist view denies responsibility for our wrong thoughts and actions, so we are not guilty before a holy God.

According to the materialist, what is the prescription for our problems? Since we are merely a collection of chemicals, chemicals will cure us. Since the immaterial or invisible world doesn't exist, there is no God or afterlife to be concerned about.

Again, please understand that we are not arguing that there are no brain diseases that can lead to disordered behavior, or that to use medicines for emotional pain is always wrong. There are also times when real brain diseases can cause us to experience emotional pain, and these often require the use of medication. We'll be exploring these subjects in greater detail later in this book.

THE COMFORT OF THE DISEASE MODEL

Most of us would prefer to think of our painful emotions as having a physical origin, rather than as being rooted in our hearts. The implications of your view on this are very important: If your suffering results from your own thoughts and choices as well as from your physical state, then you must be part of the problem. It's very difficult for any of us to admit that!

We may prefer to believe that we are suffering from an illness, because if this is the case, there is little we can do that will change our condition. At first, believing this may make our problem seem less overwhelming because it places the responsibility for change outside of us rather than inside. But in the long run, such a perspective leads to a sense of powerlessness and despair because we have to rely upon something outside of ourselves to give us hope. And what if the medicines don't work as we hoped they would? This occurs more often than most women realize.[6]

Even more importantly, if we do not see ourselves as being able to solve our problems through the grace and power of God, we have missed one of the main themes in the Bible: God enables His people to live victoriously even under very difficult circumstances.[7] Believing that we cannot change our situation by changing our lives causes more problems than it solves. When we accept the disease model as an explanation for our painful emotions, we have, in essence, concluded that the Bible consists of inspiring stories but does not offer practical help that relieves our suffering. The problem here is that the Bible clearly teaches that it *does* have solutions. Second Timothy 3:16–17 (ESV) tells us that "all Scripture is breathed out by God and profitable for teaching, for reproof, for correction, for training in righteousness; so that the man of God may be adequate, equipped for every good work."

In other words, the Bible is able to reprove and correct us and equip us so we can serve God more effectively. If we believe that what God's Word says is true, then we can't conclude that it doesn't provide help for the problems we face.

The disease model, then, excludes the Bible as a source of help. If you are a Christian, you probably want to address your pain using answers that are founded upon your faith. That's what this book is about. In chapter 2 we'll talk about the uses of medicines and help you understand how to make the best choices for your specific situation. Then in the chapters that follow, we will outline practical principles from God's Word that will help you seek God's solutions for the problem of emotional pain.

HOW THE BIBLE INFLUENCES US

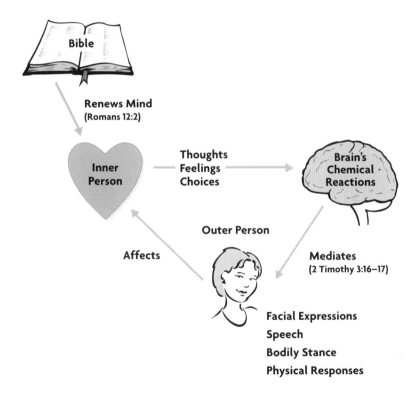

The Bible helps to direct our inner person and shape our thoughts, feelings, and choices.

CAN I REALLY CHANGE?

By now you may be feeling a little overwhelmed. You have learned that drugs do not take care of the cause of emotional pain; they only decrease the awareness of it. You have also learned that the Bible offers help for dealing with emotional pain.

You may be thinking that the Bible is fine for those whose problems are not so great, but that your problem is different and requires stronger action. Perhaps you are already taking some drugs. Maybe you have placed your faith in medicines, and you're wondering whether it's really possible to do otherwise. Or, maybe you're not sure your faith is strong enough to enable you to solve your problems without medicine.

While any decisions you make regarding medication should always be made in consultation with your physician, there is great wisdom in researching your options and seeing if perhaps you've overlooked solutions that might work better for you. It is our hope that this book will encourage you to consider the possibilities.

As for the Bible's power to change lives, we find countless evidence of this in the pages of Scripture itself. For example, the Bible's "Hall of Faith Chapter" (Hebrews 11) lists people who persevered through difficult situations by looking to God in faith. These people were like us—they were ordinary people who did extraordinary things because they trusted God. For example, Joseph was a slave who spent years in prison. He trusted and obeyed God and after much suffering became a great leader in the land of his slavery.

Rahab was a prostitute. Who knows what secret humiliation she endured? But by God's grace she trusted in Him and became an honored ancestor of Jesus Christ (Joshua 2:1–22), as did Ruth, who belonged to a despised people and was widowed at a young age. Her faith made her one of the great ones (Ruth 4:13–17). Abraham and Moses, who were fearful by nature, trusted God in difficult situations too (Romans 4:3; Hebrews 11:27) and were transformed into men of faith.

These faithful believers, and many others like them (Hebrews 11:32), experienced the emotional pains of fear, worry, uncertainty, depression, homelessness, enslavement, shame, and the threat of death. They endured their sufferings without drugs, and their faith is held up as an example to us. So can emotional pain be overcome with God's help? The answer is clearly yes. And the power that helped the people in Hebrews 11 walk in faith is the same power that's available to you today.

GROWING IN YOUR FAITH

1. Have you been tempted to think of your painful emotions as having a physical origin over which you have no control? Can you see that they could be originating in your heart?

2. Can you begin to own your feelings by changing the way you think in response to them? For example, instead of thinking, *Rainy weather depresses me,* you can think, *I'm tempted to feel downhearted when it rains.* Commit yourself to thinking honestly about your emotions this week, and journal the changes you decide to make in your thought habits.

3. A helpful exercise for personal growth is to summarize what you have learned from a chapter right after reading it. Then later on, you can look back over your notes and remember what you learned. Why not do that now? In four or five sentences, summarize the main points of the chapter.

TWO

WILL MEDICINE HELP MY PAIN?

KEEP YOUR HEART WITH ALL DILIGENCE, FOR OUT OF
IT SPRING THE ISSUES OF LIFE.

Proverbs 4:23 (NKJV)

CHAPTER 1 MAY HAVE RAISED some questions for you. You may be wondering, *You've told me that my emotional pain comes from my inner person. But I need to take blood pressure medicine, and it's the medicine that makes me feel tired and depressed. Surely that's not an inner-person kind of problem!* Or, *My doctor says my emotional problems may be causing my physical sickness. So how does that work?*

Earlier, we learned that our body and our inner person can interact with each other. In this chapter we're going to look at some of the health issues a woman may face because of this connection. We'll also examine how medicines can affect our emotions, and what we can expect from medicines used to treat our emotional pain. We'll talk about how medicines can change the way we feel, and we'll consider another approach to handling our negative emotions.

HOW OUR BODIES AND EMOTIONS INTERACT

There is a close interconnection between our inner person and our physical body. They affect each other in many dramatic ways. Our inner person can affect our physical health, and our physical health, in turn, can influence our thoughts, emotions, and choices.

The Heart Affects Our Physical Health

The physical changes that take place when a woman becomes a habitual worrier is one example of how the thoughts of the heart can affect our physical health. Worry often causes sleep loss, and the resulting tiredness can make us more prone to depression, which may diminish our body's ability to fight off infection. Worrying also increases the fight-or-flight hormone, adrenaline, which our bodies produce when under stress. A high level of adrenaline induces a restless feeling that increases our nervousness. That nervousness can then generate more hormone release, causing yet more restlessness. This can become an endless cycle, and high blood pressure, heart disease, panic attacks, depression, and frequent illnesses are some of the long-term effects of worry.

HOW YOUR HEART
AFFECTS YOUR BODY

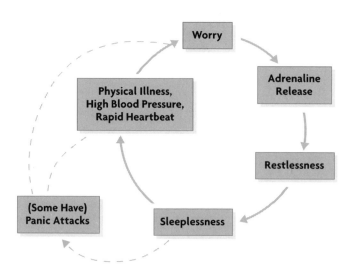

When we allow worry to fester in our heart, we set off a chain of reactions and responses that affects the body, which, in turn, can cause even more worry.

Physical Health Affects the Heart

One example of how our physical health can influence our inner person is the way that a long-term sickness can lead us to become depressed or discouraged. Physical pain or tiredness can also induce emotional reactions such as depression, even when there are no other stresses present in our lives. And pain medication can have the side effect of clouding our thoughts, which may make it harder for us to cope with our feelings. This, in turn, can result in struggles with depression or fear.

HOW YOUR BODY
AFFECTS YOUR HEART

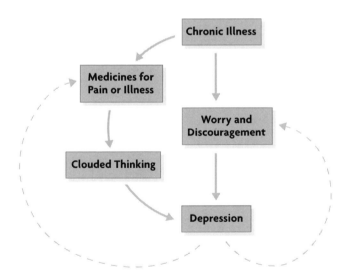

When we experience chronic illness, it can spur worry or discouragement, which in turn can lead to depression. Medicines taken for pain or illness can cloud our thinking, leading to depression, and depression can cause us to worry even more.

Lifestyle Choices Affect the Heart

Another cause of depression or anxiety can be our lifestyle choices. We can become tired, depressed, and underweight when we exercise too much. On the other hand, we may find ourselves anxious, depressed, and overweight if we get too little exercise and have poor eating habits. Failing to keep regular hours and get enough sleep at night can also provoke or worsen anxiety and depression.

Medicines for Physical Problems Affect the Inner Person

Many medicines used to treat illness can cause depression, anxiety, or mood swings. These side effects can also be caused by pain medicines, psychiatric medicines, herbal supplements, alcohol, and street drugs. Drinking too much coffee or tea may stimulate physical changes, including a faster heartbeat, which can trigger anxious feelings in some women.

Hormones Affect the Heart

Women who are in their reproductive years experience the challenges of the monthly menstrual cycle and pregnancy. The hormonal changes that occur during menstruation and pregnancy may make some women feel more emotional. Postmenopausal women may have a harder time sleeping and have lower energy levels (even in the absence of disease), and these conditions may worsen a tendency toward depression or anxiety. We will examine hormonal problems in more detail in chapter 7.

A Good Attitude Can Affect Our Health

The communication between our body and our heart can have positive effects too. A good attitude can help mend even serious physical problems. For example, Proverbs 17:22 tells us that "a joyful heart is good medicine," while Proverbs 14:30 notes that "a tranquil heart is life to the body." Even secular physicians have come to recognize the positive effect of inner-person attitudes on physical health.[1] How much more should this be true for those of us for whom "the joy of the Lord is [our] strength" (Nehemiah 8:10)!

In summary, then, real physical consequences can result from the interaction between our body and our inner person. This means that to be as healthy as we can, we need to:

- pay attention to what we are choosing to think in our hearts;
- understand that we may have more difficulty with our emotions if we are sick or taking certain medicines;
- make wise lifestyle choices if we want to remain emotionally stable.

WHAT MEDICINES ARE GIVEN FOR EMOTIONAL PAIN?

There are a large number of medicines available for those who suffer emotional pain. This is a big topic, and we can offer only a quick overview here with an eye toward understanding how they work and how the physical changes they produce may affect our heart, behavior, and other parts of our body in unintended ways. The medicines can be divided into two main groups based upon what they do: 1) drugs that improve feelings, and 2) drugs that clear confused thinking.

DRUGS THAT IMPROVE FEELINGS

Drugs that can change our feelings may allow us to feel less depressed or anxious, even if we continue to live in the same difficult situation that caused our problem to begin with. Such drugs can be divided into two subgroups: those that relax us, and those that relieve depression.

Drugs That Help Us Relax

Many of the substances that relax us are not usually used as psychiatric medicines. These include pain medicines (by this we mean strong medications for serious pain, such as Oxycontin, Vicodin, Percocet, Demerol, and Ultram, and not anti-inflammatory drugs such as those used for arthritis, including Motrin or Celebrex), street drugs, and alcohol. There are antianxiety drugs that may be prescribed as psychiatric medicines. Pain and antianxiety medicines are prescribed for different reasons and have different effects, but they both produce a relaxed feeling. Of course, some street drugs and alcohol produce relaxation too.

The problem with relaxant-type drugs is that they affect the way you feel without changing the problems that caused those painful emotions in the first place. Instead of experiencing sorrow or anxiety in response to your circumstances, you'll simply feel more relaxed. This relaxation (although it will make you feel better) won't help you resolve the root cause of the problem or help you learn how to respond to your situation in a godly way. In fact, just the opposite will happen: You'll no longer have the painful feelings that help motivate you to change or to help others change. In addition, because the medicine has masked the negative feelings that should motivate you toward change, when you go off the medication, the negative feelings will return.

Pain Medications

Although we don't think of pain pills as medicines for painful emotions, they are often given to women who are troubled by their feelings (at the time of this writing, some common medicines in this category are Oxycontin, Vicodin, Percocet, Demerol, and Ultram). Remember that our physical state can affect our emotions, and our emotions, in turn, can affect our physical state. Those who are in pain are often depressed or anxious. Those who are depressed or anxious often experience their physical pain more severely than those who do not have these feelings. As a result, physical pain and uncomfortable emotions often occur together, and pain medicine is commonly given when both are present.

Pain medicines work by *decreasing the awareness of pain in the brain*, and they produce relaxation along with the pain relief. However, they can also cause confusion, which can trigger or worsen depression and anxiety. Others find the relaxing effect of their medication so pleasant that they have trouble decreasing their dose as their emotional health improves. These pleasant sensations can tempt us to take more than we really should.

This doesn't mean that if you have been taking pain medicines for a long time you no longer need them, or that you're a drug addict. But sometimes women who have emotional issues along with their pain do develop problems with addiction. Why is this? Sometimes it can be hard to tell the difference between physical pain and emotional distress, especially if you are experiencing both of them at the same time. In addition, the Bible says we *all* have difficulty with being honest with ourselves because our hearts are easily deceived (Jeremiah 17:9). Because of these tendencies, we may find ourselves continuing to take a medicine that makes us feel better emotionally even though we no longer need it physically. I (Laura) felt the strength of this temptation when I experienced severe pain following a bad wrist fracture a few years ago.

We must hasten to add, though, that those who have never had serious pain can easily underestimate the difficulties that it can produce. It can be hard to know with certainty how much pain medicine we really need. But because the desire to stay on the medicine longer than necessary can be strong, we need to try to be suspicious of our motivations, and to remember that we will have a clearer mind and be more able to cope with our problems in a godly way if we take as little medicine as possible for as short a time as possible.

Alcohol and Street Drugs

Alcohol and street drugs are similar to pain medicines in the way they work, although they provide less pain relief and more relaxation. The pleasurable relaxation they induce can result in substance-abuse problems, just as prescription pain medicines can. And like pain medicines, street drugs and alcohol (used to excess) may make us feel better for a while, but they always worsen anxiety and depression in the long run because of the confusion of mind that they can produce.

Antianxiety Medicines

Drug companies have developed medicines that are able to relax anxious people without as much of a "high" as is produced with alcohol or street drugs. These drugs are referred to as tranquilizers because their purpose is to calm an anxious person (presently, drugs in this group include Valium, Xanax, and Ativan). Antianxiety medicines were more widely used in the 1960s and 1970s, but they fell out of favor when it was discovered that they are very habit-forming.

More recently, antidepressants that have antianxiety effects have been developed (such as Zoloft, Paxil, and Prozac). These were marketed as not being habit-forming when they were first released, but experience with these drugs has shown that they too can produce dependency.[2]

The basic problem with any drug that has a relaxing effect is that you'll need to continue using it if the situation that originally prompted the anxiety doesn't change. Remember that anxiety is a "warning light" that God designed to tell us that we have a problem. Because taking a drug for a bad feeling enables us to bear the pain without changing either our situation or our response to it, the problem producing the anxiety will undoubtedly continue. And as time goes on, the dosage of medicine needed to relieve the anxiety will also increase.

Of course, the higher your dosage, the stronger your dependence on the medicine will become. And as dependence develops, the drug's effect will seem less relaxing over time, leading you to take additional medicines or increase your alcohol intake. That's why it's not unusual for women who have been anxious for a long time to be on a number of drugs, including pain medicine and tranquilizers, and to be using alcohol or street drugs as well.

You may be thinking, *Oh, great! You're telling me that the medication that makes me feel comfortable is going to increase my problems in the long run. Now what can I do?* But we're not telling you to just stop using what may seem the only route to peace you've been able to find so far. Instead, we want to encourage you to find a way to deal with the cause of the problem and not just the resultant feelings. And, we want to help equip you to produce the godly fruit in your life that we know you want. In the Bible, God has given us very specific guidance on how to handle worry, panic, and related problems, and we'll examine this in more detail in chapter 6.

LEARNING FROM OUR PAINFUL EMOTIONS

When we face difficult circumstances that prompt painful emotions, we can opt to seek God's help, which results in growth, or we can use medicines, which might relieve the emotional pain but do not resolve the underlying problem.

Antidepressants

Antidepressants work by altering the chemicals in our brain to relieve the pain of depression. In the same way that relaxant-type drugs change our feelings without changing how we respond to difficult circumstances, antidepressants produce a feeling that doesn't match our real-life situation. It is true that sometimes the mere act of seeking help or taking medication for depression can change a difficult state of affairs simply because others finally realize how unhappy we've been and their response helps change our situation. But when our circumstances or our response to our circumstances hasn't changed, the medicine merely enables us to ignore a situation that *needs to change.* As with relaxant-type drugs, sooner or later we will need more medicine in order to continue feeling better if nothing else in our life changes.

Remember what we said about God's purpose in giving us emotions? He's equipped us with the ability to experience emotional pain so that we can understand our heart. You can see, then, how a problem can arise when we seek to deaden this pain instead of addressing the desires, wrong thinking, or distorted attitudes that may be driving the pain. And then instead of learning God's lessons from our suffering and embracing godly change, we find ourselves stuck in the same difficulties for months or even years.

"Poop-Out," Tail Chasing, and Dependence

One of the problems that we mentioned with relaxants can also occur on antidepressants. Many women find that after a period of time on a particular antidepressant, the brain fails to respond to the dosage originally prescribed to them. Doctors sometimes refer to this as "poop-out." When this happens, the dosage is usually increased, or a second drug is added. A second diagnosis, such as bipolar or anxiety disorder, may be given to explain the apparent setback, and additional drugs may be prescribed for the new disorder. It is not unusual for women who have been depressed for a long time to carry several diagnoses and be on a number of drugs, each of which can have its own harmful side effects and interaction problems.

To give you some idea of the prevalence of "poop-out," Dr. Joseph Glenmullen offers these statistics:

> Systematic studies are confirming what has been seen clinically and are finding that the [antidepressant] drugs will wear off in at least 30–40% of patients. One such study . . . found Prozac wore off in 34% of patients. Most of the patients (83%) responded to an increase

in the dose. . . . Within a year, however, the higher dose had worn off in 27% of patients. These patients required an additional increase in their dose or had to be switched to multiple other medications in the search for an antidepressant that might work.[3]

"Therapeutic tail chasing" is our term for what happens when a depressed woman develops side effects *caused* by her antidepressant. These side effects may be mistaken for symptoms of a new disorder, and more medicines may be prescribed. These extra medicines can have their own side effects, resulting in the prescription of even more medicines, and so on.

In addition to these problems, the same dependency that can develop during drug treatment for anxiety can also occur while on antidepressants. If you want to understand more about the problem of dependency, please refer to appendix B, where you'll also learn about other side effects associated with the long-term use of these drugs.

Violent and Suicidal Thoughts

I (Laura) believe that the processes of "poop-out" and "tail chasing" led me to being diagnosed as bipolar, and ultimately to my close call with murder-suicide. They may have contributed to Bill's suicide as well. A large number of studies have linked antidepressants with suicidal thoughts and a greater tendency to act upon them.[4] Antidepressants have also been linked to violent thoughts accompanied by seemingly irresistible compulsions to act upon them—even if such thoughts and behavior are inconsistent with a person's character prior to receiving these medicines.[5]

In 2004 the Food and Drug Administration (FDA) required "black box" warnings of suicide danger for children and adolescents to be placed prominently on the product labels of these drugs. "Black box" warnings are applied to drugs that have been approved by the FDA but later found to pose serious health risks. These warnings probably will be extended to adult patients following an FDA review of all the clinical studies of antidepressant treatment in adults.

We have counseled many women whose medicines produced more

problems than the original conditions that they were prescribed to treat! Once a woman has been on these drugs for a while, it becomes very difficult to tell which symptoms are caused by her painful emotions and which are caused by the medicines given to treat the emotions.

DRUGS THAT CLEAR CONFUSED THINKING

The drugs that clear up confused thinking consist of two main groups: antipsychotics and mood stabilizers.

Antipsychotic Medicines

Antipsychotic medicines are given to people who are diagnosed as having psychosis, or serious confusion in their thoughts. (At the time of this writing, drugs in this group include the newer antipsychotics such as Zyprexa and Risperdal, as well as older ones such as Haldol and Prolixin. The newer antipsychotics are rapidly replacing the older ones because they have fewer side effects.) Psychosis is usually diagnosed when a person hears voices and believes "crazy" things. Antipsychotic medicines are also sometimes given to people whose behavior or emotions are out of control. For them, the medicine restrains emotions and behavior, which is why these medicines are described as a "chemical straitjacket."

It's interesting that while antipsychotics do actually clear the thinking of persons with psychosis, their side effects cloud the thinking of those who aren't psychotic. These drugs can produce a feeling of improvement even for those who don't have "crazy" thoughts, but they do so at the cost of blunting emotions and damping down responses. They can literally restore the sanity of a person who has psychosis, but they can have serious negative effects on those who do not. If you struggle with "crazy" thoughts or you are hearing voices, or if someone you love does, you'll want to read more about this in chapter 8.

Mood Stabilizers

Mood stabilizers are medicines that were first used in persons with psychosis *accompanied by* unstable emotions (these medicines include Lithium, Tegretol, and Depakote). This combination of problems is

WILL MEDICINE HELP MY PAIN?

usually called manic depression or bipolar disorder. A person with acute mania (a psychosis with excited emotions) might believe that she can fly and end up leaping off a tall building to her death.

The diagnosis of bipolar disorder has been applied more recently to persons with unstable emotions *without* psychosis. This is what happened to Bill and Laura. Mood stabilizers can be lifesaving in cases of true manic excitement, but they can have serious side effects in those who are not suffering from this problem. We'll discuss this further in chapter 7, where we will also look at what God's Word says about the control of unstable emotions.

THE BOTTOM LINE ON MEDICINE

Because we've covered a lot of ground, let's summarize what we've learned about medicines so far:

- Many medicines and other substances make you feel better by covering up your painful feelings.
- Medicines that make you feel better can also cause dependency problems.
- Medicines that make you feel better for a while might not continue to do so unless the dosage is increased or other drugs are added.
- Medicines that make you feel better may also produce side effects that can be mistaken for new disorders.
- Violent and suicidal thoughts and actions can result from using antidepressants.
- Antipsychotic medicines can restore the sanity of those who have psychosis, but can act as "chemical straitjackets" in those who do not have this serious problem.
- You can be encouraged to know that God's Word provides real answers for women who are struggling with their emotions.

WHAT ABOUT CHEMICAL IMBALANCE?

In recent years you may have heard about medicines that supposedly treat "chemical imbalances" of the brain by remedying the serotonin levels in our brain. Even though there's been much publicity and even more advertising about these supposed chemical imbalances, there is *no evidence that our disturbed emotions are caused by a specific imbalance of chemicals in our brain.* Psychiatrist David Healy observes, "It is now widely assumed that our serotonin levels fall when we feel low. . . . But there is no evidence for any of this, and nor has there ever been. A huge gap has opened up between what is scientifically demonstrable and what people believe."[6] The next time you hear a commercial for a psychiatric medicine, listen carefully to the wording. You'll notice that no affirmative statements are actually made, but rather, words such as *may* and *might be* are employed to describe the presumed effects of the medicine.

Many mechanisms have been proposed over the years to explain the effects of psychiatric medicines, but psychiatrists no longer believe that these medicines work simply by correcting an excess or deficiency in a brain chemical.[7] It does seem to be true that increasing or decreasing the amounts of a chemical in the brain can produce improved thoughts or feelings. But exactly why this happens has not yet been well explained.

WHAT MEDICINE CAN AND CANNOT DO

As you seek to make wise decisions about whether or not to take medicine, one question you will want to ask is what you can expect a medicine to do for you. Medicine can suppress hallucinations, which are things we might see or hear that aren't really there. Medicine can decrease anxiety or improve our feelings. There are real chemical changes that occur in our brains when we take psychiatric medicines, and these chemical changes often make us feel better.

If a woman is struggling with life-threatening behavior or suicidal thinking, medicine should be used to bring her situation under control. This does not necessarily mean that the behavior or thoughts are a disease requiring drug treatment, but rather, that medicine may help calm her down, clear her thinking, or relax her so that she doesn't harm herself or others.

But there is another side to all this, as illustrated by the story about Bill and Laura. Psychiatric medicines can help suppress bad thoughts and feelings, but they can also produce changes in the brain that can lead to even worse problems than the ones that led a person to take the medicines in the first place. These medicines may change an individual's brain structure and function over time. Recent research suggests that some drugs may even rewire the brain as they produce relief of symptoms. The problem is that we don't really understand enough about how the brain works to be certain that this rewiring is good. It is possible that the use of these drugs may result in unexpected changes in other areas of our brains, which may or may not be beneficial. If this is true, it is a strong argument for not using these medicines unless a serious condition exists that can't be treated in any other way.[8]

Even more important than what a medicine can do for you is what it *can't* do for you. These failures are indeed significant:

- Medicine can't teach us to choose to think thoughts leading to peace and happiness instead of thoughts leading to anxiety or depression.
- Medicine can't show us how to make lifestyle choices that will help keep our body healthy.
- Medicine can't reveal how to respond to physical limitations with attitudes that build us up instead of tearing us down.

We believe medicine may be needed for the control of a few serious brain conditions. However, even those who take these medicines can learn self-control and thought habits that will lead to greater emotional stability through the transforming power of the Holy Spirit and God's Word.

Before you choose to take any medication, you'll want to be sure that it is the best choice for your long-term welfare. And even if you do decide to take medicine, you'll still need to work on making choices that will produce the peaceful fruit of righteousness in your life (Hebrews 12:11).

HOW DOES APPLYING BIBLICAL PRINCIPLES HELP?

As you will learn in more detail in the second part of this book, the Bible teaches that as we change our habits of thought and the choices we make, our emotional responses also change. This, in time, leads to our feeling better. Maybe you are already familiar with this truth. But did you know that our thought habits and our choices also can change our brain's structure and function over time?

When a woman is pregnant, doctors warn her to be extremely careful about what medicines she takes because the child's brain is developing. But many of us don't realize that a large body of research—in the field of *neuroplasticity*—shows that even adult brains change throughout life as a result of the things we learn and the thought habits we practice. When we return to college after our children leave home, or we take up a new activity, our learning produces measurable changes in the brain that reflect our new knowledge or skill. Even people who have suffered brain damage in adulthood due to injury or stroke have been able to "retrain" the healthy parts of their brain to help take over functions lost by the injured parts of the brain.[9]

We believe that, generally speaking, these results from secular research are consistent with the biblical truths we present in this book. Remember that in chapter 1 we showed from God's Word that as we change the thoughts of our heart, these changes could be reflected in our brain function. Well, recent research has in fact linked counseling that teaches people to change their thoughts with measurable changes in their brain's function.[10] Other studies have shown that medicines are not clearly superior in comparison to counseling that is designed to teach people how to change their thoughts.[11] These secular results affirm the value of a biblically based approach.[12]

As we practice biblical principles, we introduce changes in our lives that spring from a changed heart and can result in measurable changes in our brain function. This is very different from feeling better because a medicine has altered our brain's function by changing its chemicals in the absence of genuine heart transformation. More importantly, what medicines cannot do for us, God's truth can. Medicines can't teach us to think differently; they can only suppress the feelings we have in response to our thoughts. But God's Word can teach us to think differently, leading to feelings of joy and peace instead of depression or anxiety.

EXPERIENCING TRUE HEART CHANGE

Some women may find that change seems impossible to achieve. If that is true for you, perhaps you have not yet experienced the transformation that makes biblical change possible. The Bible tells us that we must first be "born again" to experience the power that enables us to live differently. If you are not sure what this means, please turn to appendix A, "How You Can Know If You're a Christian," to learn how you can become a follower of Christ.

Even if you are already a Christian, change can be slow and difficult, and fighting to achieve a transformation of heart can be daunting. But the Bible promises that, through Christ's power, you can change. When you're lagging in your resolve, you can remind yourself of the great love of God in Christ and in His promise that through His strength you can do everything He calls you to do (Philippians 4:13). Keep looking to Him in faith!

GROWING IN YOUR FAITH

1. Do you have physical problems that might be influencing your feelings? Are you taking medicines that you think could be making your painful emotions harder to cope with? Have you had a complete physical in the last two years? Make an appointment with your doctor to discuss the possibility of changing, decreasing, or stopping your medicines, and to ask about a diet and exercise plan. Don't forget to include daily vitamins in your discussion.

2. Do you have guilt and remorse over past sins? Don't wait another day to get right with God. If you are not sure how to do this, start with appendix A, "How You Can Know If You're a Christian."

3. Are you on psychiatric medicines or pain pills that you think you might not really need? Don't just stop taking them. First, read the rest of this book and get biblical counseling. If you decide you would like to try to stop using these medicines, then discuss this with the doctor who prescribed the medicines to you. Do not attempt to stop taking your medication without consulting your doctor.

4. Summarize, in four or five sentences, what you've learned in this chapter.

Kei's Story

When I began taking antidepressants, I was a stay-at-home mom of three young children, had a beautiful home, my husband had a great job, and we were both active in our church. From all appearances my life was picture-perfect. But inside, I felt as though I were dying. Responsibilities that other women fulfilled with ease were much more difficult for me. And feelings of sadness and hopelessness always accompanied me throughout the day.

My husband worked long hours, and I spent those hours longing for him to come home. Sadly, my craving his company had much more to do with the help that I desperately wanted rather than a desire to spend time with him. On days when he arrived home even a few minutes late, I became bitterly angry and disappointed. This put tremendous stress on our relationship, and he soon dreaded coming home at all.

As the turmoil in our home increased, so did my feelings of hopelessness. Nothing in my life made sense. I was confused and angry that God was refusing to answer my prayers to make the pain go away, and I began to believe He was punishing me for the sinful life I lived before becoming a Christian.

I didn't consider suicide, but I did wish I could just go to sleep and not wake up again. My husband became concerned and asked if I was willing to see a counselor with him. Although I felt sure that I was beyond help, I reluctantly agreed.

The counselor immediately diagnosed me as having severe

depression. At last I felt maybe I wasn't such a bad person after all—I had a disease! The counselor referred me to a psychiatrist, who immediately put me on an antidepressant.

At first I did seem to feel better, but as time went on I still struggled to love my husband and children, still lacked the joy that I so desperately craved, and experienced constant frustration and anger. I began to wonder if the medication had stopped working, and decided to stop taking it when my prescription ran out.

That's when I discovered the addictive nature of antidepressants. The severe headaches, body aches, cold sweat, and nausea that left me bedridden had me on the phone with the doctor begging for another prescription. After beginning the medication again, I felt as though I were trapped on a merry-go-round that wouldn't stop to let me off. It seemed as if I couldn't live with the medication, but I couldn't live without it either.

In the months that followed I began pouring out my heart to the Lord. This time I didn't ask Him to make the pain go away. Instead, I asked Him what I was missing. He used the truths in Scripture to remind me of who I am in Christ. I was reminded that I was fearfully and wonderfully made (Psalm 139:14), and that His grace and power were sufficient to overcome my weaknesses (2 Corinthians 12:9).

As these truths took hold in my heart, I again desired to be rid of the antidepressants. This time I weaned myself from them over a period of weeks rather than all at once. I also asked God to give me faith and strength to do what I believed He wanted for me to do.

Eventually I came to see that my "disease" was not in my brain, as my counselor suggested. Rather, it was in my heart, and the Bible defined it as sin. My problem did not originate with an imbalance in my brain's chemistry; it originated with wrong, sinful thinking that led to wrong, sinful actions. When I began to acknowledge my weakness (2 Corinthians 12:10), trust not in my own understanding (Proverbs 3:5), take my thoughts captive (2 Corinthians 10:5), and turn from my wicked ways (2 Chronicles 7:14), I began to experience what no amount of medication could give me—joy in the Lord despite my outward circumstances!

At times I still struggle with feelings of sadness and hopelessness. But I also know that nothing in this life is too big for God's grace to cover. When my mind is fixed upon this unchanging, objective truth rather than my own changing, subjective feelings, the joy of the Lord is truly my strength (Nehemiah 8:10). It is then that I can see the challenges of each day not as circumstances that threaten to crush me, but as opportunities that allow me to experience more of God's faithfulness.

THREE

LORD, WHY DO YOU LET ME HURT?

WHY ARE YOU IN DESPAIR, O MY SOUL?. . . HOPE IN
GOD, FOR I SHALL AGAIN PRAISE HIM.

Psalm 42:5

UP TILL NOW, you may have thought about your emotional pain as something that didn't really have much to do with your faith. It was just a dysfunction in the wiring or chemicals in your brain and didn't really involve your understanding of God, His plans, or His power. In some ways, viewing emotional pain as a materialist can be more comforting (at least on the surface) than the belief that God is sovereignly ruling over how you're feeling and that He is using your feelings for His purposes. But by now we can see that our emotions were given to us by God, and that it's His purpose to use them in our lives. How does that make you feel? We can imagine that right now your heart may be vacillating between two conflicting emotions: fear and hope.

THE FEAR OF CHANGE

Learning to think about life in a new way can be daunting. We all have favorite ways of comforting ourselves, of dealing with our problems with familiar strategies, and of looking at our difficulties. Given enough time, we may learn to live with our pain. Though such coping may not be effective, because we're familiar with it, we are reluctant to try alternate solutions such as those found in the Bible. In fact, perhaps the mere thought that God is at work in your emotions makes you want to run and hide. You may feel as though you are being put on trial, or exposing yourself to just another opportunity to fail.

We also recognize that the thought of having to do the hard work of pursuing change can be discouraging. Please let us encourage you in this chapter (and in the ones to follow) that you really can have hope. God has led you here, to this book, at this time, and we know that He will use it in your life for His good purposes. God hasn't deserted you in your pain. *His plans for you are good.* In fact, one Puritan writer said, "[God] will use you only in safe and honorable services, and to no worse an end, than your endless happiness."[1] He really is interested in your happiness, dear reader. But sometimes (as you're discovering) the road to happiness and joy frequently leads us through the valley of the shadow of death. We've both walked down that road, and we've heard noises in the shadows and seen sights that have threatened to terrify us. But we've also learned that God will stay with us the whole way through. We've learned to say:

> Even though I walk through the valley of the shadow of death, I fear no evil, for You are with me; Your rod and Your staff, they comfort me. You prepare a table before me in the presence of my enemies; You have anointed my head with oil; my cup overflows. Surely goodness and lovingkindness will follow me all the days of my life, and I will dwell in the house of the Lord forever. (Psalm 23:4–6)

What benefits can you know in the midst of your pain? Right now, as you read this, God is with you. The knowledge that He is with you and will guide you can bring wonderful comfort. *You don't need to fear.* He's going to feed you, anoint you, and superabundantly bless you—right in the midst of your pain. He has surrounded you with

His goodness and lovingkindness, and when He's finished with the work He's planned for you here on earth, you can be assured that His mighty power will be strong enough to bring you home to Himself. And you will dwell with Him *forever!* It's because of these truths that we can tell you not to be afraid. You don't need to trust in us, in your family members, or in your best friends. You don't even need to trust in your own ability to carry on in the fight. Trust in God and rest in His mighty hand. He will do His work; He will bring you to a place of endless happiness and peace—and all for His glory.

THE HOPE FOR CHANGE

Although this new way of looking at your problems may be making you uncomfortable, it's probably also filling you with some glimmers of hope. Perhaps you're beginning to see that you won't have to think about yourself as a person who has some strange and incurable physiological problem that will continue for the rest of your life. Perhaps you're seeing that there really is hope for you and that you're not all that different from many others. Perhaps as you've considered what we've had to say, you're experiencing a growth of faith in your heart. You might be thinking, *You mean I don't have to live like this? You mean I can be more like other Christians?* We hope that's where you are, but even if it isn't, don't worry or be afraid. Remember that God is with you, and He is committed to using the resources of heaven to help you.

ALL GOD'S CHILDREN CAN CHANGE

If there's one truth the Bible makes vividly clear, it's that we all can change. In fact, the Bible is the story of how God works in His children's lives to make them like Jesus Christ, the Son He loves. Everywhere we look in Scripture, we see encouragements to trust God, the atoning death of the Son, the power of the Spirit, the truth of His Word, and the strength of the church, His family. Think about the people whom God changed for His glory:

- He changed Abraham from a lying idolater into the "father of our faith."
- He changed Jacob, the scheming supplanter, into Israel, a prince with God.
- He changed Rahab from a harlot into a faithful woman, ancestor of King David and Jesus Christ.
- He changed Saul, the self-righteous persecutor of Christians, into Paul, the apostle to the Gentiles.
- He changed Peter from a fearful people-pleaser into a faith-filled martyr.

If God was able to bring about dramatic changes in all those people, fallen people like us, then He is able to change you too. This is how Paul put it in 1 Corinthians 6:

> Or do you not know that the unrighteous will not inherit the kingdom of God? Do not be deceived; neither fornicators, nor idolaters, nor adulterers, nor effeminate, nor homosexuals, nor thieves, nor the covetous, nor drunkards, nor revilers, nor swindlers, will inherit the kingdom of God. *Such were some of you;* but you were washed, but you were sanctified, but you were justified in the name of the Lord Jesus Christ and in the Spirit of our God. (1 Corinthians 6:9–11, emphasis added)

Look again at the list of people above. Surely, if God was able to change them through His justifying and sanctifying power, He's able to change us too. His power hasn't diminished, nor have His purposes varied. He's still in the business of conforming us to be more and more like His Son. So why not stop right now and pray? Thank God that He's making His truth and power known to you. Ask Him to help you believe that He can work in your life and that He will guide you, in His time, to the peace and joy that will glorify Him most.

WHY DOES GOD ALLOW PAIN?

We recognize that the struggle you're facing right now is hard for you. We also recognize that you may end up continuing to struggle with your pain and trials for years. We really do know that pain and sorrow, fears and disappointments are part of what it means to live here in the "not yet." That's where we're living too. Although we fully believe that God *can*, and indeed *may*, completely deliver you from your emotional pain, we also know that sometimes it serves His purposes for you to continue experiencing struggles. Why does God seemingly change some people "overnight" while He calls others to faithfully toil on month after month, or year after year? We don't know the answer to that question—it's been hidden in God's secret counsels. What we do know, however, is that He's given us His Word, and instead of trying to figure out what He's doing in every individual's life and why, we need to pursue what we do know of His plan for us (Deuteronomy 29:29).

Although God doesn't usually reveal to us exactly what He's doing in our lives, He has let us know, in Scripture, some general purposes for allowing suffering. In the rest of this chapter, we're going to try to discern some of God's reasons for our pain. It's important that we do this because we have to view our suffering the way He does. Failure to understand and "get on board" with God's purposes in our lives will result in continued difficulties, not the least of which are confusion and doubt.

Here's the reality: *God doesn't view our pain the same way we do.* We think about pain from the very minuscule yet exceedingly important perspective of our own limited experience. We think that we shouldn't have to suffer, that all suffering is bad, that a pain-free life is God's plan for everyone. Because we subconsciously hold to such beliefs, when suffering comes to us, especially in the form of painful emotions, we respond by trying to circumvent or escape the suffering in any way possible as quickly as possible. Please don't misunderstand—we're not saying that you shouldn't respond to your painful emotions. *What we're saying is that sometimes God's good purposes in our difficulties are viewed by us as something to flee from instead of something to learn from.* In fact, sometimes the very way that He answers our prayers for growth is in the form of our greatest trials.

This is how He, in His wisdom and love, has fixed the world and our lives to run, and we need to trust that the One who created us and knows us intimately knows best how to change us and fill us with His endless joy.

YOU DESERVE HAPPINESS

Recently, on a "home makeover" show, we heard an interesting comment. When explaining how the project team had built a large and elaborate entertainment room for a family, one of the team members said, in essence, "We've built this great room for you guys because you really deserve it!" Although it is good for us to help those who have fallen on hard times, there is nothing in Scripture that supports the idea that anyone "deserves" an elaborate entertainment room with all the most modern gadgets. Let's face it: The advertising executives on Madison Avenue have sold us a bill of goods, and we frequently allow Madison Avenue's messages to shape our beliefs without giving those messages much scrutiny. Do we believe we "deserve" a pain-free life filled with all the most current toys? Is that what the Bible tells us to expect? We know the answer to that question, don't we? The Bible doesn't tell us to expect pain-free lives. Rather, it tells us to expect suffering:

- *To you it has been granted for Christ's sake, not only to believe in Him, but also to suffer for His sake* (Philippians 1:29).
- *Even if I am being poured out as a drink offering upon the sacrifice and service of your faith, I rejoice and share my joy with you all* (Philippians 2:17).
- *Consider it all joy, my brethren, when you encounter various trials* (James 1:2).
- *Blessed is a man who perseveres under trial; for once he has been approved, he will receive the crown of life which the Lord has promised to those who love Him* (James 1:12).
- *You have been called for this purpose, since Christ also suffered for*

you, leaving you an example for you to follow in His steps (1 Peter 2:21).

• *Even if you should suffer for the sake of righteousness, you are blessed* (1 Peter 3:14).

The thought that pain-free living should be ours blinds us to the wonderful blessings that come to us hand in hand with afflictions. There is much good that God bestows on us through our trials, and it's important that we not seek to short-circuit His loving plan for us. Instead of focusing on whatever picture you might have of what a blessed life "ought" to look like, why not dedicate yourself to cultivating a more God-centered and realistic view of life? Remember, God will never withhold from you something that you need, nor will He take from you something you can't serve Him without.

So let's begin now to examine why God allows trials, pain, sin, and trouble. You'll come to learn that God allows (and even uses) suffering for His own glory. You'll also discover that God allows us to experience troublesome feelings so that we'll be driven to Him and to His Son. And you'll see that God allows us to suffer so that we will love Him more fully and appreciate more fully the sacrifices Jesus Christ made on our behalf (points that we will examine in the next chapter).

GOD ALLOWS EMOTIONAL SUFFERING FOR HIS OWN GLORY

When pondering the meaning of life, the Puritans in the 1600s asked the question, "What is the chief end of humanity?" In asking this, they were really saying, "What is this all about? What is the goal? What should Christians be focused on?" The way they chose to answer that question is quite enlightening. They said, "The chief end of man is to glorify God and enjoy Him forever."[2]

That's probably not the answer you would get if you interviewed most people today. The Puritans lived in an era full of suffering (including persecution against them), and they believed that everything, including suffering, happened for one purpose only: *God's own glory* (and in His glory, our enjoyment). The Bible bears this out in many places, including Romans 11:36: "For from Him and through Him and to Him are all things. To Him be the glory forever. Amen."

Think about those words. *Everything* is about Him! Just as the slogan goes, "It's Not About Me." That little saying really does get to the heart of what both Paul and the Puritans said. *Everything is from Him and through Him and to Him and for His own glory!* We know that *glory* is one of those words Christians have overused, and thus it has become somewhat meaningless. But when the Bible talks about God's glory, it has two rich layers of meaning. The first layer is the "praiseworthiness of the Creator; layer two is the praise which this draws from His creatures."[3] Why do we experience trouble and suffering here? So that we will see how great and praiseworthy God is, and so that upon seeing this greatness, we will give Him the praise He deserves.[4]

Now we come to a very difficult question: How does your suffering bring glory to God? In fact, it might seem to you that your suffering is the last thing He should choose to use to glorify Himself. Wouldn't God be more exalted and praised if our lives were free of suffering? Although this seems reasonable, this logic is flawed. It is flawed because *the chorus that exalts God when our lives are pain-free is a faint shadow when compared to the deep, resonating hymn of faith that is distilled from the crushed soul* of a Job who sings, "As for me, I know that my Redeemer lives, and at the last He will take His stand on the earth. Even after my skin is destroyed, yet from my flesh I shall see God" (Job 19:25–26).

What would we know of God's ability to sustain, guide, and comfort us if we had never felt the crushing of life's dearest pleasures or trod the gloomy path that led through the valley of the shadow of death? Even the beloved apostle Paul knew of this truth when he wrote:

> I am convinced that neither death, nor life, nor angels, nor principalities, nor things present, nor things to come, nor powers, nor height, nor depth, nor any other created thing, will be able to separate us from the love of God, which is in Christ Jesus our Lord. (Romans 8:38–39)

Paul savored the magnitude of God's love for him in Christ in the midst of intense personal suffering. In the same way, our suffering and trouble teaches us about God's great power, endless compassion, and sustaining grace in ways that we would never learn nor treasure otherwise.

THE WITNESS OF OTHERS WHO HAVE SUFFERED

Aside from the testimonies of Job, David, Paul, and the Puritans, consider the suffering of more modern-day saints such as Joni Eareckson Tada and Corrie ten Boom.[5] Joni suffered a neck injury as a young woman and has since spent her life in a wheelchair, paralyzed from the neck down. Her testimony to Christ's sustaining power and wonderful grace has encouraged many people, particularly those with physical handicaps.

Corrie ten Boom grew up in Holland during World War II. Because her family provided a safe hiding place for Jews fleeing from the Nazis, they were eventually arrested and confined to concentration camps. Her story of faith in the midst of intense personal suffering serves as an inspiration to many people today. When we think of these women's woes in light of the faithful praise and worship that exudes from their hearts, we begin to get a clearer perspective of how much greater God is than anything this world might try to sell us on—even the thought of a pain-free life.

The Lord will become sweeter and more beautiful to you as He uses your troubles to strip away the scales that blind your eyes from beholding His true beauty. He's teaching you that temporal happiness is nothing in comparison to the glory that is yet to be known by us. God allows emotional suffering to continue in this world because it glorifies Him to do so.

GOD USES SUFFERING TO BRING US NEAR

C. S. Lewis wrote that God whispers to us in our pleasures and shouts to us in our pain.[6] Although most of us want pain-free lives,

God has obviously decreed that pain-free living isn't best for us. It is true that God has placed within us all the desire for the happiness that pain-free living seems to promise. Our problem is not with our desire for the happiness of ourselves and others. The problem that we have is that we think that true happiness comes from someone or something other than God.[7] God's goal is that we experience true, endless happiness, and He knows where that happiness and joy come from. True happiness and joy come as we are changed to become more and more like Christ. God's goal in our suffering is to make us more like His Son, as Romans 8:28–29 teaches:

> We know that God causes all things to work together for good to those who love God, to those who are called according to His purpose. For those whom He foreknew, He also predestined *to become conformed to the image of His Son.* (emphasis added)

God wants us to be like His Son so that we'll find the real joy He's lovingly planned for us. It's easy for us to think that we would be completely whole and satisfied with life in the here and now if everything would just line up with our wishes. But it's in the very withholding of our desires (even those that seem good in themselves!) that the Lord lovingly teaches us the deeper delights found in Himself.

In addition to this compassionate sharing of Himself with us, God also uses our suffering to woo us closer to His heart. Frequently we don't recognize our great need for Christ or our great need to rely on God until we're faced with a difficult circumstance or uncomfortable emotion. Our unhappy feelings tell us that there's something wrong with life as it is here, and that's just what God wants us to learn. God is speaking loudly to us in our pain. Do you hear what He's saying?

The writer of Psalm 119 echoed these thoughts in several verses. Let's consider some of them:

- *It is good for me that I was afflicted, that I may learn Your statutes* (Psalm 119:71). What is God teaching you through your affliction? What are you learning about His Word? Can you see any way in which your trouble has been good for you?

- *Before I was afflicted I went astray, but now I keep Your word* (Psalm 119:67). Has the affliction you've gone through with your emotions helped you to become more obedient? God's purpose in your suffering is that you learn to obey Him, no matter how you feel. He's also using your troubles to tether you closely to Him so that you won't go astray. Have you looked at your pain in this way? Is God using your suffering to keep you close to Himself?

- *I know, O Lord, that Your judgments are righteous, and that in faithfulness You have afflicted me* (Psalm 119:75). Do you know, in your heart of hearts, that God's judgments and laws are completely and always right? More pointedly, do you believe that His dealings with you are honorable and upright? Do you believe that His plan for your life is beyond reproach? Has He not only been faithful to stay with you in your affliction but also in afflicting you so that you would know and love Him more deeply?

- *I am exceedingly afflicted; revive me, O Lord, according to Your word* (Psalm 119:107). The psalmist experienced exceeding afflictions, but he looked to the Lord to revive him through His Word. In the past, you may have tried to find scriptural help to revive you, and that's part of what we'll do together in this book, but what we want to ask you now is this: Is God's Word the source of your strength today? Do you ask Him to illuminate your heart to His Word so that today, and just for today, you'll have the revived heart that you'll need to make it through?

RESPONDING TO YOUR SUFFERING IN FAITH AND HOPE

As we come to the end of this brief discussion on suffering and God's uses of it, let's look at two more passages of Scripture. First, let's listen to these words from Paul:

In this house we groan, longing to be clothed with our dwelling from heaven. . . . For indeed while we are in this tent [he's referring to his physical body], we groan [he's referring to his inner person], being burdened. . . . Therefore, being always of good courage . . . *for we walk by faith, not by sight* . . . we also have as our ambition, to be pleasing to Him. (2 Corinthians 5:2, 4, 6–7, 9, emphasis added)

Paul was burdened and felt crushed in his inner person. Have you ever felt burdened and crushed? But even though Paul was suffering so, he didn't allow his feelings to dictate his faith or his actions. Instead, he chose to "walk by faith" and live his life out (even in his suffering) seeking to please God. The psalmist expressed the same determination in Psalm 42:

Why are you in despair, O my soul? And why have you become disturbed within me? Hope in God, for I shall again praise Him for the help of His presence. O my God, my soul is in despair within me; therefore I remember You. . . . Why are you in despair, O my soul? And why have you become disturbed within me? Hope in God, for I shall yet praise Him, the help of my countenance and my God. (verses 5–6, 11)

The psalmist's experience of despair was real, but it wasn't more real than his faith. He believed that God would help him because God was near to him. He determined to remember God, and he believed that one day his countenance would change. He believed that a time would come when he would again praise God and his feelings would be lifted up. Not only did the psalmist force his faith to inform his emotions, he also let his faith correct the wrong thoughts his feelings were producing. He asked himself, "Why are you in despair? Why have you become disturbed within me?" His faith worked to remind him that what he was experiencing today was not necessarily what he would experience tomorrow. He also remembered that his emotional experiences were not necessarily speaking the truth to him about God and his situation. And so, he placed his hope in God's ability to help him.

As we end our time together in this chapter, let us ask you: Do you have hope? Do you believe that the God who promised He would never leave you nor forsake you is *with you right now?* Do you believe that though you feel afflicted and discouraged, the living God who loves you with the same love He lavishes on His Son (John 17:23) will strengthen, enlighten, and encourage you?

Even if your honest answer to these questions is no, don't despair. God is stronger than your emotions and is able to pull you up out of the miry pit. Trust in Him and remember that you're not alone in this. He's right there with you, and He won't leave.

When we struggle with our emotions, the only sure footing that we can find is in Scripture. Ultimately it really doesn't matter that our friends are encouraging us or that we've convinced ourselves that we are getting better. What really matters is that God is there, understanding, upholding, protecting, and pitying us. So even if you don't feel like doing the study questions that follow, just start with one question and read the Scriptures . . . and then move on, as you are able, to the next. We know God will be faithful to meet you.

GROWING IN YOUR FAITH

1. One of God's good purposes in allowing you to suffer is for His own glory. What do you think this means? The following verses are meant to direct your thoughts about God's purposes in your trials. We realize we've listed quite a number of them, but we want to encourage you to take time to look them up so that you can better understand God's intent to glorify Himself in your life: Psalm 115:1; Isaiah 42:12; Luke 2:14; Romans 11:36; 16:27; Galatians 1:4–5; Ephesians 3:21; Philippians 4:20; 1 Timothy 1:17; 6:16; 2 Timothy 4:18; Hebrews 13:21; 1 Peter 5:11; 2 Peter 3:18; Jude 1:25; Revelation 1:5–6; 4:10–11.

2. Read aloud Psalm 42 now, using it as a prayer for God to help you, comfort you, and cause you to praise Him once again.

3. The Lord's plan is for you to grow in faithful obedience *no matter how you feel.* What can you do today that would demonstrate your willingness to walk by faith and not by sight? (For further study see Deuteronomy 8:3; Romans 8:24–25; 2 Corinthians 4:17–18; 1 Peter 1:6–8; 5:8–11.)

4. Let's consider believers who struggled with two painful emotions: fear and despair. Abraham dealt with fear (Genesis 12:11–13; 20:2), as did Jacob (Genesis 31:31; 32:7), Moses (Exodus 2–3), Elijah (1 Kings 19), and the apostle Peter (John 18:25–27; Galatians 2:11–12). The Psalms were written by people who struggled with despair, discouragement, and doubt. Consider, for instance, Psalms 35:14; 43:5; 55:4–5; 61:2; 142:2–3; 143:3–4. What do those references teach you about the emotions of some well-known believers? What does this tell you about your own experiences?

5. Summarize, in four or five sentences, what you've learned in this chapter.

Kelly's Story

I have suffered from depression since my teen years, and did not realize my problem until I began marriage counseling with my husband during the first few years of our marriage. I had much difficulty facing life's challenges and was consumed with hopelessness and self-pity on most days. Our therapist, who was not a Christian, thought antidepressants would help me.

But the medication made me worse, not better. I was still the same old me with the same old habits—nothing had changed. My marriage and my relationships with my child and stepchildren suffered a great deal because of my depression. I had what was called self-destructive behavior. I became numb to the depression and slowly began to believe there was no way out, so I didn't care about the consequences of my behavior. In fact, I thought the world would be better off without me.

I never got close to suicide, but it seemed like an appealing option at times. God allowed me to stumble and hit rock bottom to get my attention. The consequences were severe and the pain was vast, but God knew it would take something devastating to bring me to the place of surrender. I almost lost my marriage in the spring of 2003, and if it hadn't been for the Holy Spirit and His divine intervention, I would have. I knew I needed a miracle.

In summer of 2003, I reached out to a woman who now is my mentor, spiritual mom, and friend. I shared with her a brief history of my life, the devastations in my marriage, and my struggle to love Jesus. I asked her if she could mentor me. She said yes gladly and with great enthusiasm.

By November I was pregnant with my second child. Although my husband and I had not planned for this child, apparently God had! This pregnancy forced me to quit taking antidepressants. I now was dependent on God's forgiveness and redemption. He knew my faith would be strengthened if I depended on Him and not the medication.

In January 2004 I joined a Bible study led by my mentor, and we studied Nancy Leigh DeMoss's book Lies Women Believe and the Truth That Sets Them Free. *During this study God revealed everything behind my depression, beginning with how it all began. I saw how the lies of the Enemy had structured my life and had caused my depression, which required a heart change, and not medication. The changes in my life are a testimony that God can cure any person who suffers from depression and fill one's heart with hope—all without drugs!*

I began to identify the lies of the Enemy and combat them with God's truth. I wrote specific Scriptures on index cards and memorized them. As I battled depression, I responded by thinking and doing the right thing even when I didn't feel like it, and having faith that God would meet me where I needed Him.

My mentor shared with me the example of Moses. Moses had to stretch out his arm over the Red Sea before God parted it. As Moses acted out in faith, God did the rest. For me, this meant just getting out of bed in the morning and trusting God to give me the energy to face the day. And this really does work! I began to do what was right even when I didn't feel like it. I began to sow good seeds, and God began to change my heart.

Now my husband and I are deepening our love through forgiveness and grace, my relationships with my stepkids are more than ideal, I have a newfound love for my first daughter and treasure my second one, and I enjoy loving my family and giving them all I have.

Yes, at times I still struggle. But it is in my struggles and my weakness God works His miracles best. This only causes my faith to grow and to love Him more. Praise God for the tough times!

FOUR

LORD, WHY DID YOU HURT YOUR SON?

YET IT WAS THE WILL OF THE LORD TO CRUSH HIM;
HE HAS PUT HIM TO GRIEF.

Isaiah 53:10 (ESV)

BEFORE THE RELEASE of Mel Gibson's movie *Passion of the Christ*, there was a lot of heated debate about whether the movie was anti-Semitic or not. Some people charged that Gibson was trying to portray the Jews as "Christ-killers." Others, in trying to defend Gibson, pointed out that the Romans were just as culpable. All during these discussions, the astounding reality about who was ultimately responsible for the death of Jesus seemed to be concealed to many. The truth about the passion of the Christ is that ultimately it wasn't the Jews or the Romans or even all of sinful humanity that brought about the death of the Son of God. *It was God Himself.*[1]

This is the astonishing truth about the suffering of our Savior. His suffering wasn't imposed upon Him by any earthly person. He wasn't afraid of what the Jews or Romans might do to Him. This is what He said: "No one has taken [my life] away from Me, but I lay it down on My own initiative" (John 10:18). Even at His crucifixion Jesus knew that all the power of heaven was His if He chose to defend Himself:

"Do you think that I cannot appeal to My Father, and He will at once put at My disposal more than twelve legions of angels?" (Matthew 26:53). If Jesus had wanted to protect Himself, He certainly could have done so. Yet He submitted Himself to the powerful plan of His sovereign Father, which was that He would die on the cross to redeem humanity.

Isaiah chapter 53 is a particularly powerful passage affirming that the crucifixion was God's work. We would strongly encourage you to read the entire chapter slowly and thoughtfully before you continue reading. And note especially verse 4: "Surely he has borne our griefs and carried our sorrows; yet we esteemed him stricken, smitten by God, and afflicted" (ESV).

Verse 10 goes on to add, "It was the will of the Lord to crush him; he has put him to grief" (ESV). Though Christ died for our sins, it was God who brought about the crucifixion. There is a lot stated in Isaiah 53 about our dear Savior, and we can summarize it with these points:

- He was despised and rejected.
- He was a man of sorrows.
- He knew about grieving.
- He was wounded, crushed, and chastised.
- He was beaten and oppressed.
- He was in anguish.
- He was oppressed.
- He was falsely judged.
- He had no beauty or majesty.
- No one esteemed Him.

What thoughts do these words put in your heart and mind? Have you thought deeply about Christ's sacrifice and wondered why He should suffer in this way? Does His suffering speak to you at all in your pain? We know that it would be very easy to say something like, "Sure, Jesus suffered, but what does that have to do with me and my suffering?"

Our goal in this chapter is to bring to you the grace and comfort that the Lord intends for His children to have. Although the grace-filled comfort that you may be desiring probably seems, in some ways, disconnected from the suffering of your Savior, please drink deeply of the thoughts to follow. Christ's suffering really does relate to yours, as you'll soon discover.

WHY HIS SUFFERING MATTERS TO YOU

If you're a Christian, Christ's suffering really does matter to you, at least on some level. Apart from His death, burial, and resurrection, you don't have any hope for peace with God or justification. In order for a person to become a Christian, he or she must believe that Christ's suffering was something more than a nice gesture or a good life-example to follow. His suffering was necessary for our salvation because we are all guilty before a holy God and deserving of His eternal judgment. In His suffering, the Lord bore the punishment for our sins and transferred to us His perfect righteousness. Isaiah spoke of this transfer of suffering and blessing in this way:

> He was WOUNDED *for our transgressions;* he was CRUSHED *for our iniquities;* upon him was the CHASTISEMENT that brought *us* peace, and with his STRIPES *we are healed.* All we like sheep have gone astray; we have turned every one to his own way; and the Lord has laid on him the *iniquity of us all.* (Isaiah 53:5–6 ESV, emphasis added)

Even though Christ lived a perfect life, He had to suffer and die under God's wrath so that we could have a relationship with His Father and the resulting forgiveness, peace, and healing that we desperately needed. *He took our place in His execution, so that we might take His place in our adoption.* (If this idea is new or unclear to you, please turn to appendix A, where we discuss this in greater depth. Jesus' desire is not merely that you learn to cope with your painful emotions in a more "healthy" way. Rather, He desires your salvation and complete peace with God.[2])

HOW DOES CHRIST'S SUFFERING RELATE TO MINE?

While we can see why Christ's suffering was important for our salvation, it's a bit harder to understand why His suffering is important in our day-to-day struggles with emotional pain. For some of us, His suffering might seem like a nice but distant reality that doesn't really relate to figuring out how you're going to make it out of bed and off to work for another day. But it's true—Christ's suffering doesn't merely affect your eternal destiny. *His suffering can lift your burdens and strengthen you right now—today!* His suffering:

- Gives you the grace you need to walk by faith in your suffering
- Gives you confidence that He's with you in your pain
- Brings meaning to your suffering
- Demonstrates His great love for you
- Assures you that there will be an end to your suffering

Let's take a closer look at each of these points and see what we can learn about the great assistance our Lord offers to us.

His Suffering Brings You the Grace You Need to Walk by Faith

God's grace to us is an important factor in facing suffering—a factor that is often overlooked. The word *grace,* in the New Testament, is the Greek word *charis.* This wonderful word is used of "the merciful kindness by which God, exerting his holy influence upon souls, turns them to Christ, keeps, strengthens, increases them in Christian faith, knowledge, affection, and kindles them to the exercise of the Christian virtues."[3]

Author Jerry Bridges defines God's grace in this way:

Grace, as used in the New Testament, expresses two related and complementary meanings. First, it is *God's unmerited favor to us through Christ whereby salvation and all other blessings are freely given to us.* Second, it is *God's divine assistance to us through the Holy Spirit.*[4]

Christ's suffering brings us unmerited favor, delight, joy, and happiness that not only opens the door for the salvation of our souls, but also supplies us with everything we need to persevere through our sufferings. In fact, your suffering is one of the primary ways that God opens your heart to understand how much He's given to you through Christ's suffering. In your suffering you've begun to learn how much you need Him; you've begun to see the error of self-sufficiency. Because He's suffered for you, you're now able to grasp the wonderful truth of your complete dependence upon Him. If He hadn't suffered in your place, you would just continue to believe that life would work out if you just tried harder. But that's not the truth. The only assurance that we have that life will "work out" is because of Christ's sacrifice and suffering. He suffered so that you will have the grace and strength you'll need when your suffering makes you see yourself as weak and helpless. Instead of militating against weakness, we should embrace it (in some ways) as God's good gift to us to open our eyes to all that's been given to us in Christ. Paul began to taste this as he suffered with his "thorn in the flesh." Although we don't know exactly what Paul's thorn was, we do know that Paul learned something new about Christ's grace from it. This is what he wrote:

> He has said to me, "My grace is sufficient for you, for power is perfected in weakness." Most gladly, therefore, I will rather boast about my weaknesses, so that the power of Christ may dwell in me. Therefore I am well content with weaknesses, with insults, with distresses, with persecutions, with difficulties, for Christ's sake; for when I am weak, then I am strong. (2 Corinthians 12:9–10)

Paul learned that Christ's power was most known to him (and through him) when he was weak. Christ suffered so that Paul (along with us) would know the blessing in weakness. After all, what could be weaker than a bruised, naked man, nailed to a cross, waiting to die? And yet think of the miraculous power that pours forth from that sight!

It's easy for us to minimize Paul's suffering and think, *It really wasn't that big of a deal for him. After all, this is the apostle Paul we're talking about here. How much could that "thorn," whatever it was, have really bothered him?* But that's not the picture that Paul paints for us. He called the thorn a "messenger of Satan" that "tormented" him. This tormenting wasn't a little concern or troubling annoyance. In the original Greek text the word translated "tormented" means "to strike with clenched hands, to buffet with the fist."[5] Paul was battered by this affliction, and it made him feel weak. Paul was so concerned about this weakness that he prayed three times that it would leave him. He probably would have continued to pray for release from it if the Lord hadn't spoken to him: "My grace is sufficient for you, for power is perfected in weakness." The Lord understood that there was something about His power and grace that Paul would never learn about if the apostle felt strong and in control. Consequently, Paul's suffering was really a blessing to him. His weakness resulted in greater strength and kept him from feeling proud and self-sufficient.

This is really antithetical to our way of thinking today, isn't it? We twenty-first-century Christians are all about self-help and conquering weaknesses and difficulties. We are unaware that God wants to teach us holy lessons about Himself through our affliction. Is there something here that we've missed in our race to self-perfection? Suffering opens you to an experience of grace that is more than you'd know if you had not suffered. Do you desire to know the Lord more? Do you want to share in the rare depth of strength that comes straight from the throne room of heaven? This kind of strong grace doesn't come to those who don't need it. It's a precious gift for those who are weak and desperate. The Lord comforted Paul by telling him that His grace—*and just His grace*—was enough for him. Will it be enough for you?

Perhaps the Lord will ultimately deliver you from the weaknesses and afflictions you're facing right now. It's proper to hope and to pray in that direction—after all, both Jesus and Paul did. But what if that's not God's plan? Do you believe that even if you have to continue on in suffering, you can find the strength to do what He calls you to do every day? His grace is powerful enough to blast right through all of your doubt, fear, and hopelessness and to write on your heart, *He's enough for me.* He suffered so that you would be qualified to savor this truth: He's enough for us all.

His Suffering Assures He Is with You in Your Pain

Unlike man-made deities, Jesus Christ is the only God who suffers *with* His people and has even entered into their suffering. Although Jesus existed in perfect harmony and bliss in fellowship with His Father, He entered into a physical body (for all eternity) so that it might be said of Him that He was a merciful and faithful high priest:

> He had to be made like His brethren in all things, so that He might become a merciful and faithful high priest in things pertaining to God, to make propitiation for the sins of the people. (Hebrews 2:17)

He was made just like you so that He would be able to pay the price for your justification. He was also made to be just like you, with the capacity to suffer, so that you would know He understands what you're going through and be assured that He can indeed help you:

> Since He Himself was tempted in that which He has suffered, He is able to come to the aid of those who are tempted. . . . Therefore, since we have a great high priest who has passed through the heavens, Jesus the Son of God, let us hold fast our confession. For we do not have a high priest who cannot sympathize with our weaknesses, but One who has been tempted in all things as we are, yet without sin. Therefore let us draw near with confidence to the throne of grace, so that we may receive mercy and find grace to help in time of need. (Hebrews 2:18; 4:14–16)

Think about this: the Creator of the universe was hungry (Luke 4:2) and thirsty (John 19:28) just like you. He mourned over the effects of sin in the lives of those He loved (John 11:33, 35; Luke 19:41). He was tempted in every way that you are (Hebrews 4:15). He lowered Himself and didn't grasp at the rights that were His as God, "but emptied Himself, taking the form of a bond-servant, and being made in the likeness of men. Being found in appearance as a man, He humbled Himself by becoming obedient to the point of death, even death on a cross" (Philippians 2:7–8).

Although Jesus was sinless, there was a sense in which even He learned obedience through His suffering (just like us today!).

> In the days of His flesh, He offered up both prayers and supplications with loud crying and tears to the One able to save Him from death, and He was heard because of His piety. Although He was a Son, He learned obedience from the things which He suffered. (Hebrews 5:7–8)

Jesus endured shame, suffering, and hostility so that we would not grow overly discouraged, and we are to look to Him as our example: "Fixing our eyes on Jesus, the author and perfecter of faith, who for the joy set before Him endured the cross, despising the shame, and has sat down at the right hand of the throne of God. For consider Him who has endured such hostility by sinners against Himself, so that you will not grow weary and lose heart" (Hebrews 12:2–3).

Because He has entered into our suffering, you can be assured of His presence with you now. He isn't embarrassed about you or disappointed in you. He's moved by your suffering and grieves over it because He knows what it's like to suffer. And He still bears the marks of His suffering today.

Each of the aforementioned passages from Hebrews is pivotal for you as you walk through your pain because almost every person who struggles with painful emotions feels isolated and alone. And even though you probably recognize the "aloneness" of your situation, you probably also cut yourself off from others because you can't stand to watch their response or because you think you don't fit in. Yet even in your solitude, you're not alone. Jesus is there with you, and He understands. He's been afflicted, betrayed, and cut off. He's felt the weight of great loss and the blows of those who should have loved Him.

His Suffering Brings Meaning to Your Suffering
If we never take time to look deeply at the cross to see the suffering

of our Lord and all that it means to us, we'll miss another one of the most precious truths about suffering—that it has meaning. We all know that the experience of suffering isn't pleasant. That's a given. But when our suffering doesn't seem to have any meaning, that surely makes it sting more, doesn't it? The truth, however, is that we don't have to live with meaningless despair. *Our suffering matters.* It doesn't have meaning only because it teaches us about Him; it also has meaning because our sufferings are somehow tied to His own. As He has shared in our suffering, so we also share in His, as these verses teach us:

- *And if children, heirs also, heirs of God and fellow heirs with Christ, if indeed we suffer with Him so that we may also be glorified with Him* (Romans 8:17).
- *We are afflicted in every way, but not crushed; perplexed, but not despairing; persecuted, but not forsaken; struck down, but not destroyed; always carrying about in the body the dying of Jesus, so that the life of Jesus also may be manifested in our body* (2 Corinthians 4:8–10).
- *To you it has been granted for Christ's sake, not only to believe in Him, but also to suffer for His sake* (Philippians 1:29).
- *Now I rejoice in my sufferings for your sake, and in my flesh I do my share on behalf of His body, which is the church, in filling up what is lacking in Christ's afflictions* (Colossians 1:24).

There is a way in which our suffering has meaning because it is tied into His and it brings glory to Him. Although this is a difficult concept to grasp, it is plainly taught, so we should seek to understand it. When the Bible says we are suffering with Him or are filling up what is lacking in His suffering, it doesn't mean that His sufferings are not efficacious for our salvation. When in agony Jesus uttered the words, "It is finished," *it really was.* But when the Bible says that we are suffering with Him or completing His sufferings, we must understand it to mean that there is something in our sufferings that brings the gospel or God's purposes to others in a way that cannot happen apart from our troubles. Just as we are one with Him in His resurrection, so we are one with Him in His suffering. We do not suffer as He did—our suffering is not meritorious, it doesn't earn us any special favor with God. But God does ordain that our suffering be used in His sovereign plans and purposes. In this light, our trials become something more than a dark cloud that has obliterated the sun; our trials become part of God's plan to rain His truth upon the earth.

As we suffer, we must remember that our suffering is part of what it means to be a member in the "body of Christ," as one commentator explains: "Believers should regard their sufferings less in relation to themselves as individuals, and more as parts of a grand whole, carrying out God's perfect plan."[6] How does your suffering further the kingdom of God? Perhaps you can't answer that question right now. Perhaps all you can see is that others know you suffer and yet you believe—and that encourages them that there is a God worth trusting. His kingdom and glory are worth it, aren't they?

His Suffering Demonstrates His Great Love for You

The suffering of the Son should assure you that even though you may feel like a failure, and even though you may want to experience His presence and love but feel that you can't, He does in fact love you. The passage that best speaks about His love for you in your suffering is Romans 8:31–39. Though it's a long passage, you will certainly feed your soul if you take time to meditate on its powerful and comforting truths. Why not stop here and read the passage? When you finish, note that Paul asks his readers seven important questions. These questions are important for you to ponder as well.

1. *What then shall we say to these things?* What should we say about the fact that there is no longer any condemnation for us? What should we say about the fact that we've been called, justified, glorified, changed into Christ's image, adopted and assured of His help, presence, protection, and pity?

2. *If God is for us, who is against us?* Since God is the sovereign ruler and judge over all creation, who could harm us if He is for us? The suffering of Christ is the assurance that God is for us. Even

though your heart may be telling you that He isn't for you, that's not the truth. Your heart can lie to you. God is for you and He is with you—just look at the cross!

3. *He who did not spare His own Son, but delivered Him over for us all, how will He not also with Him freely give us all things?* Doesn't the suffering and death of His Son tell you something of the measure of His love? He was willing to give over for you the Son He loved. Doesn't that tell you of His immense love for you?

4. *Who will bring a charge against God's elect?* No one can bring a charge against you that will stand in the courtroom of heaven. If you are a Christian, God has justified you. He isn't embarrassed about, despairing over, disappointed in, or regretting your salvation. When Satan comes to accuse you before Him, the suffering Son proclaims, "Not guilty!"

5. *Who is the one who condemns?* No one can condemn you, because the only one who had a right to do so has already suffered in your place and pronounced you righteous in His sight (2 Corinthians 5:21). Jesus is no longer dead. Instead He has been raised and is seated at the right hand of God, interceding for you. That means that He's pleading or praying for you in the throne room of heaven. Even if you think your prayers don't have a possibility of getting answered, do you think that His prayers do? He suffered so that you can have the assurance that there is now *no condemnation* for you!

6. *Who will separate us from the love of Christ?* Because Jesus Christ has suffered for you, nothing—not even your sin, unbelief, or pain—can separate you from His love. No matter what you think or how your heart might condemn you, *no one, not even you,* can separate you from His love. No matter how you feel right now about this truth, it remains true nonetheless. If your heart tells you that He couldn't possibly love you, even then, you can know that He remains true. He suffered so that you can be assured of this truth.

7. *Will tribulation, or distress, or persecution, or famine, or nakedness, or peril, or sword separate you from Christ's love?* Maybe you can believe that no person can separate you from Christ's powerful love, but are there circumstances that might do it? No! Even if you were to

die as a martyr, His love is strong enough to sustain you into your eternal home. Perhaps you don't feel like an overwhelming conqueror right now, but His relentless grace is inescapable nevertheless.

His Suffering Assures That Your Suffering Will End

Unlike those in the world who have no hope of a future joy, Christians now have a certainty that their suffering will last only for a season. The joys that are promised to believers are meant to encourage us when it seems as though what we're going through here is more than we can stand. If we are truly His, then we can know this for certain: This is the only place where we will suffer. Because Jesus drank down *every drop* of God's wrath, we can know that there will come a time when we will bask in the sunshine of His eternal smile and pursue all of our chief joys—and all without the stain of sin. There will come a time when every tear, sorrow, and sigh will fly from your breast as an insignificant little sparrow flits across the heavens into anonymity. In place of the leaden, sulfurous clouds that are threatening to suffocate your soul, you'll find that soon you'll be able to take in great drafts of living light and you'll swim in a river that will instantaneously heal your soul and refresh your body. This transformation will be so great that the trials you're facing right now will seem to you like nothing more than "one night spent in an inconvenient motel."[7]

Sorrow is meant to draw your heart upward to your real home, heaven. You won't be disappointed there, and you'll never cry another tear nor be terrified about the future. This is the way that John, in his isolation and sorrow while in exile, described heaven:

> I heard a loud voice from the throne, saying, "Behold, the tabernacle of God is among men, and He will dwell among them, and they shall be His people, and God Himself will be among them, and He will wipe away every tear from their eyes; and there will no longer be any death; there will no longer be any mourning, or crying, or pain; the first things have passed away." (Revelation 21:3–4)

What you're suffering right now is real and it is hard, but remember, it's only temporary. A new life and new reality are on their way—life as you know it right now won't continue on like this forever. Of that you can be sure.

GOD'S PLEASURE AT CHRIST'S SUFFERINGS

Earlier, we read passages from Isaiah 53 that spoke of the Father's will in grieving and striking His Son. Your loving Father chastised His one perfect Son so that you wouldn't have to suffer meaninglessly nor perpetually. We know that you are suffering right now or you wouldn't have picked up this book, but we hope that as you've looked into the suffering of the Son, you've been able to get a new perspective on God's love, mercy, and boundless grace. How great is God's love? Look at the cross. How determined is He to bless and beautify you? Look at the cross. How sure is He that He'll be able to hold onto you, no matter what happens? Look at the cross.

GROWING IN YOUR FAITH

1. What does the word *grace* mean? How does the concept of God's grace encourage you?

2. First Peter 5:10 says, "After you have suffered for a little while, the God of all grace, who called you to His eternal glory in Christ, will Himself perfect, confirm, strengthen and establish you." God Himself has promised that He will complete the work He began in you. How does the cross testify to and certify this truth?

3. In Ephesians 3:17–19, Paul tells the Christians in Ephesus that his prayer for them was "that you, being rooted and grounded in love, may be able to comprehend with all the saints what is the breadth and length and height and depth, and to know the love of Christ which surpasses knowledge, that you may be filled up to all the fullness of God." Paul's prayer was that they would begin to experience the fullness of Christ's love. What have you learned about Christ's love in this chapter? Since Paul prayed this way, you can too. If you don't sense the Lord's smiling countenance or His immeasurable love, you can ask Him to help you do so. Don't just ask Him to cause your suffering to stop. Instead, ask Him to flood you with His love in the midst of it.

4. Summarize, in four or five sentences, what you've learned in this chapter.

PART TWO

SEEKING
ANSWERS
WITH
GOD'S HELP

FIVE

DEPRESSION: AN OPPORTUNITY IN DISGUISE

BE ATTENTIVE TO MY WORDS . . . FOR
THEY ARE LIFE TO THOSE WHO FIND
THEM, AND HEALING TO ALL THEIR FLESH.

Proverbs 4:20; 22 (ESV)

OUR HOPE IS that the first half of this book has given you a biblical foundation upon which to see your pain from a better, more hopeful perspective. In this second half, we're going to look at specific forms of emotional pain and help you apply some of the principles that you learned in the first section. We'll start in this chapter with a look at depression. And after we've taught you a new way to think about your depression, we're going to give you some concrete help on how to live in the light of your new understanding. Why not take a moment now to pray that the Lord will illuminate your heart to His truth and infuse you with His wisdom?

WHERE DO THESE FEELINGS COME FROM?

What is this depression that you feel? Sometimes it's best described as a blackness, an emptiness or hopelessness that never ends, a sorrowing without hope. It's sorrow, but it's more than that: It's the absence of any real feeling except nothingness. For many women, these feelings seem to come upon them from out of the blue. It's almost as though one day they awaken to the fact that the sun has disappeared and all the colors that used to cheer them have washed out.

REMEMBERING WHO YOU ARE

As you know, you are made up of two distinct yet interrelated parts: an outer person, or body (which includes your brain), and an inner person (what the Bible calls your mind or heart). Most secular scientists believe you're only a body, and say that the biochemical firings of your brain and the chemistry that conducts those firings are responsible for making you what you are. Are you sad? Your brain is misfiring. Do you feel as if the sun has suddenly lost its light? The chemicals in your brain are unbalanced.

It's very logical for scientists who believe in this kind of materialism to tell you that the answer to all your problems will be found in a little pill (or a combination of pills). That's because they believe there's nothing more to you than a collection of chemicals called your body, so when you don't feel well, more or different chemicals are what you need.

The Bible, and consistently biblical counselors, will point you in a different direction. They will tell you that you're not just a body, but that you also have what the Bible calls a mind or heart—an inner person who can learn, change, and grow. The biblical answers to your *heart's discomforts* are not found in a pill.

Now, this doesn't mean we (or the Bible) don't accept the appropriate use of medicines. We certainly do. But just as there can be an appropriate use of medicine, there can also be inappropriate use. When the problems we're facing have to do primarily with the body and its functioning, a medicine that cures or relieves physical symptoms is part of God's common grace to our suffering world. But when the problems we're facing have to do primarily with the heart or inner person, something different is needed. Only God can cure an ailing heart; only the Spirit can bring hope and light to a distressed mind.

IF IT'S NOT MY BRAIN, WHAT COULD IT BE?

Because your painful feelings may come from a variety of sources, let's take a moment now to consider what some of those sources might be. You may be living through a terrible tragedy or experiencing incessant disappointments. Is the life you're living now very different from the life you expected?

Perhaps your depression is a by-product of a misunderstanding of what God's Word teaches. Maybe you thought that embracing a life of faith meant enjoying a life without pain. Or your melancholy might be the result of a perceived failure to live up to what you believe others expect of you. Perhaps you're struggling under a guilty conscience and just can't forgive yourself for something you've done.

On the other hand, your distress may be coming more directly from a different source. It may be related to a chronic physical illness, persistent mistreatment of your body, or medicines that you need to take for an illness. If you buy into the belief that your depression comes from just one source, you'll limit the avenues for help and change that are available to you. Try to keep an open mind now as you work through the following pages (and questions) in an attitude of faith.

The good news about each of these causes of depression (and others like them) is that the Lord, in His grace and mercy, can renew, change, and strengthen you. And though it might not seem like it right now, this really is *better news* for you than the diagnosis of a chemical or genetic dysfunction. Although it's true that solving the above problems will require faithful work on your part, it's also true that you'll be able to experience God's grace in a new, dynamic way, and at the end of the process you'll also know Him better.

What will you learn? You'll learn about God's power to sustain a soul in the midst of suffering, and His amazing power to change hearts. You'll learn about how He suffered in your place, and you'll learn to love Him even more. Looking at your depression in this light really is better news because you'll be facing your struggle with resources superior to those that the world's largest producers of antidepressants can offer you: the atoning power of the cross, the transforming power of the Spirit, the potent illumination of His Word, and the comforting embrace of the church. Take heart, dear sister. *This really is good news!*

Let's take time now to learn more about the causes of depression that were mentioned earlier. As we do so, you'll discover some very practical helps for you. But before we begin, there's one very important thought we want to stress: If you're presently on any antidepressant medicine, *do not go off of it unless you do so under the supervision of your doctor.* It's possible to experience serious side effects from the cessation of these medicines. So if you end up thinking it's time for you to stop taking them, see your physician first, and reduce your dosage at a slow rate so as to help minimize the side effects of withdrawal.[1]

WHAT'S GOING ON IN YOUR LIFE?

Usually when we interview women who are struggling with depression, we hear a history of tragedy or disappointments, coupled with disbelief that these life-challenges are contributing significantly to the way they feel. For instance, we've spoken to women who've been in loveless marriages for years and whose children are in heart-breaking rebellion, and yet they can't understand why they're depressed. To many of these women, and perhaps also to you, the life they've lived for so long seems normal to them, and they feel as though it really isn't affecting them. So, the first question that we want to ask you is: *What's going on in your life?*

Although some disappointments might seem inconsequential to others, each of us is invested in specific areas of our life in different ways. For instance, for one woman the tragedy of being unable to bear children might be the source of her depression, while for another woman, having to resort to an epidural during the delivery of her fourth child might bring a crushing grief.

The point is this: What registers as a tragedy or disappointment for you might be very different from what would trouble another woman, so you can't compare your circumstances to those of anyone else. If you're grieved by a particular loss or circumstance, don't dismiss it too quickly as a possible cause of your depression.

Let us encourage you to stop and prayerfully reflect on your life. Are there ongoing circumstances in your life that have saddened you? After we have lived with disappointment or tragedy for a while, feeling empty or dead inside can seem normal. For some of us, this is just the way we cope with our grief—we shut down our emotions because they're too painful to face. It's almost as if we just hold our breath and hope that the pain will be over soon. This is a normal response. But remember that the pain we experience is God's gift to us to tell us that something is wrong, that something needs fixing. Instead of ignoring the circumstances (although that might be easier), you need to find God's way of handling it.

If you think that your situation is not really all that bad, why not ask a godly woman for her thoughts? Let someone who's looking in from the outside offer you a fresh viewpoint. You might ask her, "I'm reading this book about emotional pain, and I'm wondering if you think that I might be depressed because of what's going on in my life. Would you be willing to help me get another perspective?"[2]

WHERE'S YOUR TREASURE?

While you're wondering about whether your circumstances are influencing your pain, remember that life circumstances have different degrees of importance to each of us depending on our beliefs and the things we treasure most. This is what the Lord taught us when He said, "Where your treasure is, there your heart will be also" (Matthew 6:21).

What do you treasure most? What do you usually worry about? What do you think will bring happiness or joy to you? If you've been depressed for some time and you no longer are sure of what you treasure, then look back in time. In the days when you knew you treasured something, what was it?

Considering these questions is beneficial because they may help you understand the "why" of your depression. Sometimes it seems as though our depression comes to us out of nowhere, when, in fact, our depression may be telling us something significant about ourselves. Identifying your cherished treasures may help to clear up your murky thinking the way that miracle cleansers clear up muddy water. *Oh, you might realize, my depression tells me that my commitment to high standards that I can't actually achieve is causing more problems than it solves!* Perhaps your depression is God's way of telling you that your abuse of alcohol or your strong desire to look beautiful or experience romance isn't worthy of your calling as a believer.

This is the freeing truth you can learn through your depression: You weren't created to love and worship anything more than you love and worship God; and when you do, you'll feel bad. God has made you to feel pain when you've got other treasures that you've placed above Him. He wants you to treasure Him—and when you do, you'll experience fullness of joy and pleasures forever (Psalm 16:11).

WHAT IS GOD DOING IN YOUR DEPRESSION?

You can begin to wage war against your depression today by telling yourself that although it may be true that your circumstances aren't even coming close to your expectations, it's God's blessing that is letting you realize this. Instead of just seeking to feel better (something we all long for), you can tell yourself that your depression is a letter from your heavenly Father to help you draw closer to Him, love Him, and live wholeheartedly for Him.[3]

As you've thought about your unmet expectations or unfulfilled desires, what do you think the Lord wants you to do about them? Perhaps He's telling you that you need to tap into the wise resources of the church and find a godly woman who can help you identify your personal treasures and then replace them with a passion for serving others and the Lord.

WHAT DO YOU THINK GOD HAS PROMISED YOU?

Some Christians have been taught to believe that being a person of faith guarantees them a life of joy and peace. They've been taught that any sort of suffering, especially emotional suffering, means that they don't have enough faith. This toxic theology not only flies in the face of biblical truth, but is also the cause of much grief. Two good questions for you to ask yourself are, *What do I believe the emotional life of a true believer looks like? Is sadness or disappointment part of my understanding of life (albeit redeemed life) on a sin-cursed planet?*

Would it surprise you to know that many godly people in the Bible struggled with depression and melancholy? Listen to their words and see how they describe the pain they experienced:

- *Moses:* "If You are going to deal thus with me, please kill me at once, if I have found favor in Your sight, and do not let me see my wretchedness" (Numbers 11:15).
- *Job:* "Oh that my grief were actually weighed and laid in the balances together with my calamity! For then it would be heavier than the sand of the seas" (Job 6:2–3).
- *David:* "How long, O Lord? Will You forget me forever? How long will You hide Your face from me? How long shall I take counsel in my soul, having sorrow in my heart all the day? How long will my enemy be exalted over me?" (Psalm 13:1–2).
- *Jeremiah:* "My sorrow is beyond healing, my heart is faint within me!" (Jeremiah 8:18).
- *Paul:* "Even when we came into Macedonia our flesh had no rest, but we were afflicted on every side: conflicts without, fears within. But God, who comforts the depressed, comforted us" (2 Corinthians 7:5–6; see also Romans 9:1–2).

Does it surprise you that these heroes of faith all struggled with overwhelming sorrow? Experiencing heartache doesn't necessarily mean that you're not a believer or that God is somehow displeased with you. Even though our culture tells us that we have a right to be happy and feel good about ourselves, that's not what the Bible teaches. Although we do have a certain measure of joy that's unknown to unbelievers, being grieved is simply part of living in a sin-cursed world. Will there come a time when every tear will be wiped away?

Yes! But the mere fact that God will have to wipe away our tears should tell us that tears and crying are part of what it means to live here on this side of heaven.

WHAT DO YOU THINK IS REQUIRED OF YOU?

Living your life to please yourself or others may also have become a source of depression for you. If so, even your depression itself may be a cause of self-condemnation.

We believe this is one reason so many women accept the materialist perspective of their depression. Just thinking that their depression might be, in any way, a reflection of their own heart brings them more self-condemnation and guilt than they think they can bear. We know this is a very strong dynamic in the life of a woman who already feels like a failure.

If your heart is resonating with these words, let us assure you: God didn't send His Son to die for women who were perfectly whole and well. No, this is what your Savior said: "It is not those who are well who need a physician, but those who are sick. I have not come to call the righteous but sinners to repentance" (Luke 5:31–32).

And even though most Christians realize this, we somehow think that things ought to be totally different once we're saved. The truth is that we are living a new life and that the power of sin is truly broken; but abiding sin remains in us, even after our conversion, so that there is a continual war in our hearts. That's why the great apostle Paul lamented,

> For the good that I want, I do not do, but I practice the very evil that I do not want. . . . For I joyfully concur with the law of God in the inner man, but I see a different law in the members of my body, waging war against the law of my mind and making me a prisoner of the law of sin which is in my members. (Romans 7:19, 22–23)

If your heart is always condemning you, if you find that you're never able to live up to your own expectations, then depression will be an unwelcome, incessant boarder. A few good questions you might begin to ponder are:

- Whose standards are you trying to live up to?
- Are they the Lord's, yours, or someone else's?
- Can you make a list of your standards? How do they compare with God's simple requirements to love Him wholeheartedly and your neighbor unreservedly?

Sometimes grown women spend their whole lives trying to prove that they're not like their mothers or that they're as good as their mom. Do you find a dynamic like that in your heart too?

Other women live in a family context that is so shaming and critical that even though they might have had a fairly positive outlook by nature, they've now slipped into a slough of despair and everything they hear reminds them of failure upon failure.

There is good news for you. The good news is that you are now so loved and accepted, not because of any work you could do, but because of the flawless charity and mercy of your heavenly Father, that it really doesn't even matter if you or anyone else condemns you: "There is now *no condemnation* for those who are in Christ Jesus" (Romans 8:1, emphasis added). You no longer have to live for the approval of others, but can now live embracing the truth that you're in Christ and you have put on His robe of righteousness. In God's sight, you couldn't be more perfect or loved than you are.

Are you in Christ? If so, then the only condemnation that will really matter throughout eternity—the condemnation and judgment that comes from God—has already been poured out on the Son for you. You no longer have to rely upon yourself, your own merit, your own ability to approve of yourself. It's all been handled for you. You might say something like this to yourself when you're tempted to fall into the mire of self-condemnation: *It's true that I fail a lot and that I don't have anything to brag about. But God knew this about humanity, so He sent His one and only Son to bear the punishment that we deserve. Now, instead of relying on my own merit or myself for anything, I will rely on Him and believe that all the goodness, righteousness, wisdom, and strength I need will come from Him.*

FINDING REST IN HIS FORGIVENESS

Sometimes women feel depressed because they can't forgive themselves. They think, *I know God has forgiven me because I've asked Him to. But I don't feel forgiven. I know that I haven't forgiven myself, because I just can't believe that I would do something so horrible! Even though God has forgiven me, I just can't get past this failure and every time I think of it, I fall more and more deeply into a pit of despair.*

Dear sister, if that's how you've been thinking, we've got encouraging news for you: You are not commanded to forgive yourself. The Bible is clear that if we ask God for forgiveness, "He is faithful and righteous to forgive us our sins and to cleanse us from all unrighteousness" (1 John 1:9).

Of course, the sorrows that we face when we "can't forgive ourselves" come primarily from the false belief that we really should be able to do better, don't they? We think, *Now that I've been a Christian for a while, I can't believe that I still fail like this!* The liberating truth we need to embrace is that our battle with sin will remain until we're perfected in heaven. This doesn't give us carte blanche to sin, but it does inform us of the realities of life this side of eternity. God is committed to our change, but change is a slow process. God's grace will sustain us all the way, and He's committed the resources of heaven and earth to helping us.[4] When your heart condemns you, remember that "God is greater than our heart" (1 John 3:20). So who are you going to listen to?

WHAT BURDENS OF GUILT ARE YOU STILL BEARING?

Since we're already asking you to focus on your heart, please let us delve a little deeper. Are there sins you're harboring there? Perhaps there might be anger or resentment that you haven't turned from, or a self-indulgence or addiction that you both love and hate.

Are you familiar with the story *Pilgrim's Progress* by John Bunyan? The main character, Christian, carried a terrible load of guilt that threatened to crush him under its weight until it was loosened from him at the cross. Proverbs 28:13 talks about this: "He who conceals his transgressions will not prosper, but he who confesses and forsakes them will find compassion." We know that the struggle against sin can be very difficult and that the thought that you might need to confess sin and ask for help (again!) can be very daunting.

Some women may conclude that God doesn't want to hear from them or that He's tired of forgiving them. These lies flow from their Enemy, the Devil, but also from their own heart of unbelief. We know it's hard to believe that God will continue to forgive us, especially when it seems that we fail so often, but let us remind you of something that the Lord Jesus taught His disciples. In Matthew 18, He told them they must forgive their brothers "seventy times seven" (verse 22).

Think of that! We're commanded to be willing to forgive others at least 490 times—in other words, all the time. Do you think the Lord would require something of us that He's not willing to do Himself? If He commands you to forgive exponentially, do you think He does anything less? We're convinced that the Lord's forgiveness extends expansively and profoundly not only over the sins we know (and hate) but also over the sins we're not very aware of (and still love). He is a "God of forgiveness, gracious and compassionate, slow to anger and abounding in lovingkindness" who won't forsake His people (Nehemiah 9:17). Jesus is the friend of sinners. Do you sin? Then you qualify to be His friend.

WHAT'S GOING ON IN YOUR BODY?

In addition to the aforementioned possible causes of your depression, there may also be a physical cause. Have you struggled with a chronic illness or long-term pain? Do you presently take pain medications? As we've discussed before, these physical elements can and do affect the way your heart is reacting and interacting with the Lord and those around you.

The prophet Isaiah poignantly records the mourning of Hezekiah, one of the kings of the Old Testament. Hezekiah had been very ill and, of course, his illness had affected his emotions. If you're suffering pain or illness, see if this record of his experience resonates with you:

> My life is but half done and I must leave it all. I am robbed of my normal years, and now I must enter the gates of Sheol. Never again will I see the Lord in the land of the living. Never again will I see my friends in this world. My life is blown away like a shepherd's tent; it is cut short as when a weaver stops his working at the loom. In one short day my life hangs by a thread. All night I moaned; it was like being torn apart by lions. Delirious, I chattered like a swallow and mourned like a dove; my eyes grew weary of looking up for help. "O God," I cried, "I am in trouble—help me." (Isaiah 38:10–14 TLB)

Can you feel the hopelessness and sorrow Hezekiah felt because of his illness? Look at what he said next: "But what can I say? For he himself has sent this sickness. All my sleep has fled because of my soul's bitterness. O Lord, your discipline is good and leads to life and health. Oh, heal me and make me live!" (verses 15–16 TLB).

Do you find Hezekiah's perspective interesting? He believed that the Lord sent his illness and that it was for his good, even while he was praying for healing. And then, after he received God's healing, this was his response: "Yes, now I see it all—it was good for me to undergo this bitterness, for you have lovingly delivered me from death; you have forgiven all my sins" (verse 17 TLB).

God chose to heal Hezekiah, and He may do the same for you. We don't know what His plans are, but we do know that when we suffer, we can plead with Him for healing. The question that Hezekiah's testimony forces us to consider is this: Do you believe God is in control of this situation in your life? Do you believe it is for your good? Are you continuing to pray, in faith, and trust that He will heal you if it is His will?

Your Response to Sickness or Pain

If you've been told that you have a chronic or life-threatening disease or injury, don't be surprised that the news makes you feel bad. It's hard to feel happy when your world has been turned upside down, and when your physical body feels lousy.

What if you've prayed for healing, and God's answer is no or not yet? Can you feel better in your heart while your body still feels bad? Just understanding that physical pain and sickness are depressing can help you to endure them patiently as you wait for God's perfect timing. As you persevere prayerfully, understanding that it is natural to feel bad, you'll find that God ministers His grace to you, whether or not the pain stops right away. You'll come to terms with your sad news. Whether or not you get well, you'll learn to trust Him in a new way as you walk with Him through this trial.

On the other hand, you may be abusing your body, causing physical problems because you are mistreating yourself. Anorexia, bulimia, overexercise, overeating, or drug and alcohol abuse can, by themselves, cause depression, which can in turn force you more deeply into these destructive behaviors. If you're practicing any of these, you'll find your depression will grow in direct proportion to your practice of them. Rather than address these behaviors here, we'll recommend two resources you can look to for further help: For eating problems there is Elyse Fitzpatrick's *Love to Eat, Hate to Eat: Breaking the Bondage of Destructive Eating Habits* (Eugene, OR: Harvest House, 1999), and for addictions there is Edward T. Welch's *Addictions: A Banquet in the Grave* (Phillipsburg, NJ: P & R Publishing, 2001).

Here is a recap of the kinds of questions we're encouraging you to ask yourself. You may want to put a check mark by those that touch on how you are struggling:

- What's going on in your life? Are there significant disappointments, regrets, or tragedies?
- How did you think the Christian life should be? Did you believe that a life of faith meant a lack of tears?

- How focused are you on pleasing people, including yourself? Whose praise are you living for?

- What do you think God's expectations of you are?

- Do you have burdens of guilt that haven't been unfastened? Stop and confess them now. Ask God to flood your soul with new light and hope.

- Do you have any significant physical problems? Are you continuing to pray for healing? Do you see this suffering as coming from the hand of a loving Father?

- Are you taking any medications that might cause depression? Are you exercising, eating properly, resting appropriately, and taking vitamins?

As you look over the list of questions above, don't be surprised if you've checked off more than one. In fact, it's quite normal to check off all of them because they are all linked in one way or another.

WHAT IS GOD UP TO?

Since we know God is sovereign (He really is in control of everything), there must be a reason He's allowing you to go through this trial. Although we don't know the exact reasons for your suffering, let us remind you of some of the reasons for suffering that were presented in chapter 3:

- God uses suffering to draw us to Him. Ask yourself: *Have I been hiding from God, not wanting to experience more pain?* Instead of hiding from Him, why not run to Him as Hezekiah did and cry out for help?

- Through suffering we learn to be more grateful for the suffering of God's perfect Son. Ask yourself: *Has the suffering of Jesus meant more or less to me during this time?* If Christ's woes haven't become more precious to you, ask Him to make them so. Remember, "Jesus Christ did not come to take away your pain and suffering, but to share in it."[5]

- Suffering is meant, in part, to motivate us to seek to change. Ask yourself: *How willing have I been to look deeply into my heart and ask God to change me? Am I willing to ask God to change me even if that means that my suffering might continue for a while?* Sometimes the thought of having to change (particularly when it seems as if no one else is!) can be daunting. Just remember, your goal isn't to change in response to others. Rather, it's to change in response to the great love of God in Christ (Romans 5:3–5).
- Our pain works to reveal our own misconceptions and sins and to lead us to repentance and truth. Ask yourself: *Is it possible that among the reasons I'm suffering is because my thoughts about God are incorrect, or because God is trying to show me ways that I'm sinning by loving something more than I love Him?* God isn't unkind. He doesn't bring suffering or trials into our lives for the fun of it. He's working toward a specific goal: changing us into the likeness of His Son. Sometimes we're unaware of what's happening in our hearts, and the Lord, in His kindness, is seeking to reveal more truth to us through the use of our pain.
- Suffering humbles and enables us to comfort others who are suffering. Ask yourself: *How has my struggle with this trial made me more aware of my weaknesses? How has this awareness made me more gentle or humble so I can better comfort others?* God is interested in using your gifts for the betterment of His Son's bride. In going through this trial, you're being better equipped to serve others in the church who are suffering. It's important for you to remember that your suffering isn't just about you as an individual; it's about you as part of a body that needs your gifts—tempered and refined by fire as they may be (2 Corinthians 1:3–11).

INITIAL STEPS TOWARD HELP

It's comforting to know that other people have felt what we're feeling and to know that our sorrows are shared. That's what Paul was getting at when he wrote, "No temptation [or trial] has overtaken you that is not common to man" (1 Corinthians 10:13 ESV). Just knowing that we're not the only one who has ever faced a certain set of circumstances or temptations can be comforting.

At a time when the great apostle Paul was struggling with depression, he was encouraged by the presence of his friend Titus (2 Corinthians 7:6–7). Even though it is true that only God can truly bring comfort to our saddened souls, one of the means that He uses is a mature Christian friend. In the same way that Titus brought comfort to Paul, a mature sister in Christ can bring comfort, illumination, and hope to you. God has given gifts to the church so that the needs of your heart might be met through them, as Paul himself taught in 1 Corinthians 12:7: "To each one is given the manifestation of the Spirit for the common good." (If you don't have any friends to talk with, please see endnote 2 on page 230.)

Once you've found someone to walk with you through this darkness, there are several steps you can take together. First you should ask her to read through this chapter with you and help you answer the questions. Second, you should commit yourself to pray with her consistently. Ask your friend to pray with you even when you don't want to pray.

Another way your friend can help you is by listening to your perspectives and thoughts and helping you to understand and believe God's truth about suffering. She might do this simply by reading Scripture to you, or perhaps she can help you see how your thinking needs to change in response to God's Word.

At the opening of this chapter we read these words from Proverbs 4:20, 22: "Give attention to my words . . . for they are life to those who find them and health to all their body." God's Word is life and healing—no one else's words are like that! The thoughts of our own minds seem reasonable and logical until we compare them with Scripture. God can bring life and health to you through His Word, and it is sufficient to bring change to your heart. As Jesus taught, "The words that I have spoken to you are spirit and are life" (John 6:63).

As you deal with depression, know that God's Word is truer than your feelings, and it's His Word that can give you the faith and hope you need right now. And if you have a friend who can go over the Scriptures with you, she can tell you when your perspective doesn't match up to the truth of God's Word. You may also want to ask your friend to assist you as you go through some of the resources listed in appendix D, should you desire to use them.

Finally, ask your friend to help you see areas of your life where you're failing to fulfill the responsibilities that God has placed before you. For instance, if your depression stops you from caring for your family the way you should, ask her to help you determine what steps you could take beginning today to faithfully respond in obedience. Even though getting up and washing the dishes may seem to be just another meaningless exercise in futility, doing so will help you feel better and will also be a blessing to those who are relying on you. This is the very counsel God gave to Cain in Genesis: "Then the Lord said to Cain, 'Why are you angry? And why has your countenance fallen? If you do well, will not your countenance be lifted up?'" (Genesis 4:6–7).

DEPRESSION CYCLES

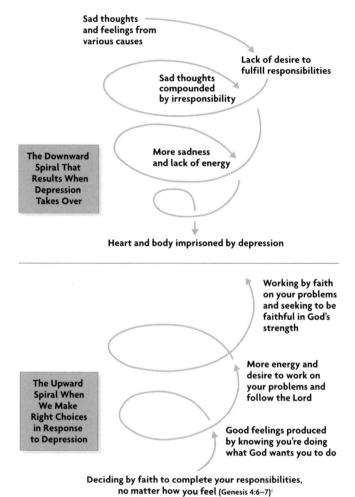

Sad thoughts and feelings from various causes

Lack of desire to fulfill responsibilities

Sad thoughts compounded by irresponsibility

More sadness and lack of energy

The Downward Spiral That Results When Depression Takes Over

Heart and body imprisoned by depression

Working by faith on your problems and seeking to be faithful in God's strength

More energy and desire to work on your problems and follow the Lord

The Upward Spiral When We Make Right Choices in Response to Depression

Good feelings produced by knowing you're doing what God wants you to do

Deciding by faith to complete your responsibilities, no matter how you feel (Genesis 4:6–7)[6]

HIS MINISTRY TO YOU

We want to close with a reminder of why Jesus came to earth:

When [Jesus] came to the village of Nazareth, his boyhood home, he went as usual to the synagogue on Saturday, and stood up to read the Scriptures. The book of Isaiah the prophet was handed to him, and he opened it to the place where it says: "The Spirit of the Lord is upon me; he has appointed me to preach Good News to the poor; he has sent me to heal the brokenhearted and to announce that captives shall be released and the blind shall see, that the downtrodden shall be freed from their oppressors, and that God is ready to give blessings to all who come to him." He closed the book and handed it back to the attendant and sat down, while everyone in the synagogue gazed at him intently. Then he added, "These Scriptures came true today!" (Luke 4:16–21 TLB)

Are you poor in spirit? He came to bring you good news. Are you brokenhearted? He came to heal you. Do you feel blind and oppressed? He came to bring you sight and freedom. God is ready to give blessings to all who come to Him! Won't you do so today? We know that you love Him, or you would not have persevered through this book as you have. The Son who went to Calvary in your place is now very near to you and offering you His hand. Will you take it?

It's very possible that His hand will take the form of a brother or sister who will walk through this process with you. After you've prayed for Jesus' guidance and help, the next step for you to take is to call your church or a trusted friend and ask for help. In the meantime, you can work through the upcoming questions, even if all you're doing is one a day. If you feel that you can't even do this, then ask the Lord to give you strength to begin to do so. And go pick up the phone. If the first person you ask isn't available to help right now, don't give up. Ask someone else![7] Remember, no matter how you feel, God's Word is true! He is committed to you and to binding up your broken heart.

GROWING IN YOUR FAITH

1. Read these examples of how other people of faith suffered: Job 17:1; Psalms 69:1–3; 119:82; 143:7–8. In what ways is your suffering similar to theirs? In what ways is your suffering different? How did David respond to his despair?

2. God has committed Himself to comforting and encouraging you. Is it a struggle for you to believe that? Please use His Word to build your faith: Romans 15:5; 2 Thessalonians 2:16–17.

3. God can bring comfort to you through others, as the following verses demonstrate: 1 Corinthians 16:17–18; 2 Corinthians 2:13; 1Thessalonians 3:2, 6–7. Ask the Lord now to give you the faith you need to go to a mature sister for help. Remember, if the first (or second) person you ask can't help you, don't give up. If you're part of a biblical church, God does have someone there for you. If you don't know whether your church is biblical or not, we've listed some questions you can ask in endnote 2 on page 230.

4. Ask the Lord to help you change your thinking. Ask Him to help you destroy false beliefs and false hopes and to put on truth instead (see 2 Corinthians 10:4–5).

5. The best avenue of victory for you is God's Word. It will help you understand your own heart (Hebrews 4:12), it is incredibly powerful (Jeremiah 23:29), it will make you adequate to do what He's calling you to do (2 Timothy 3:16–17), and it will restore, enlighten, and warn you (Psalm 19:7–11). Even though some time may have passed since you last fed your soul there, why not make a commitment to begin reading your Bible every day, even if it's only part of a psalm? If you can't remember how to pray, then perhaps you

can use the Psalms as your own prayers.

6. Make a list of the responsibilities you have been neglecting. Pick one that you'll begin doing each day for a week. Pray before you start, asking God for grace to be faithful to do your work for Him, and then start on it. Don't pick a task that will overwhelm you to begin with; rather, pick one you'll be able to complete in a short time. As you experience small successes, then take on more tasks.

7. Summarize, in four or five sentences, what you've learned in this chapter.

Kathy's Story

In 1999, I read a resource that strongly encouraged people to abstain from using any drugs that would alter their feelings. I knew the antidepressant I was taking at the time was, in fact, altering my feelings, but I quickly dismissed the advice.

Some months later, a woman in my Bible study said God could heal depression. Others agreed with her, but I became angry and exclaimed, "Not chemical depression!"

The next morning I heard a Christian Scientist say on the radio, "Christian Scientists don't believe Sarah could have had a baby at ninety years of age because biologically that wouldn't have been possible, and they don't believe Jesus could have ascended into heaven because of the law of gravity." I said to myself, "Yeah, and I said God couldn't heal chemical depression." It was at that point that I said, "Okay, God. I'm willing to try."

By this time I had been taking antidepressants and other medicines for severe depression and fibromyalgia for five years. I was on the maximum dosage of the antidepressant, so I knew I probably needed to taper off my usage of the medicine.

While I was going through the weaning process in August 1999, a good friend and I had a traumatic falling-out. She asked me to not contact her for three months. I was devastated and cried for days as I not only grieved the loss of the friendship, but anguished over other pains from the past that had been numbed by the antidepressant. During this time I cried out to

God, and His Word was a balm to my hurting soul. I also asked a friend, Holly, if I could be accountable to her about my emotions and relationships. In all this, the Lord was gracious and sustained me, and eventually I stopped taking antidepressants.

In 2001 I had a time of severe anxiety and panic attacks that lasted nearly a month. I asked people to pray for me, and consistently cried out to the Lord, asking for His help and meditating on His Word. He took me through this difficult time. When my father died on Thanksgiving Day in 2002, again I cried out to the Lord and asked friends to pray. God was sufficient for me through the sadness. He didn't take it away, but He was present with me.

Through all this I was greatly comforted by Psalm 91:4: "Under His wings you may seek refuge." In the same way a baby bird hides under the shadow of his mother's wings for protection, I could hide under the protective care of the Almighty God of the universe. All I had to do was rest!

I went through heart surgery in 2004. Depression is a normal physical response for a person who has had this procedure, and a physician in my church encouraged me to get into God's Word during that time and to be confident that I would make it through. Though doctors wanted to prescribe an antidepressant for me, by the grace of God, I was able to say no.

I still struggle with bouts of sadness and anxiety at times, but the Lord continues to minister to me through His Word, my accountability partner, and others who lift me up in prayer. I understand now that everyone gets sad or depressed at one time or another, and that we have the choice to stay in the pit of despair or to cry out to God and find His comfort. I've learned that when I seek God, the depression always passes.

SIX

CASTING ALL YOUR ANXIETY ON HIM

THEREFORE HUMBLE YOURSELVES UNDER THE
MIGHTY HAND OF GOD, THAT HE MAY EXALT YOU AT
THE PROPER TIME, CASTING ALL YOUR ANXIETY ON
HIM, BECAUSE HE CARES FOR YOU.

1 Peter 5:6–7

LIKE DEPRESSION, fear is a warning sign meant to help you, even though this might seem hard to believe if your fear feels out of control. Yet the ability to experience proper fear is a gift from God. Imagine what life would be like if we weren't able to identify real danger and then prepare for it. God gave us the ability to recognize peril and protect ourselves (and others), and He made the accompanying physical experience of fear uncomfortable enough to call us to action.

Remember what we've said about the interaction between our heart or mind and our physical body? It's very easy to see how they interrelate when we think about the process of fear. For instance, let's suppose your car has stalled at a railroad crossing and you can hear a train whistle in the distance. Quickly, your mind grasps your perilous condition and transfers this reality to your physical brain. Your brain then registers this fear and dispatches impulses to various other parts of the brain and then to the rest of the body. In a matter of milliseconds, your body releases adrenaline, the fight-or-flight hormone (as well as other chemicals), and your heart rate, eyesight, and blood flow all change. This hormonal response is a well-known experience, and we've all heard stories of people who moved extremely heavy objects when under the influence of this hormone. Your body's ability to respond to danger, then, is God's good gift to you.

HOW OUR BODY RESPONDS
TO THOUGHTS OF DANGER

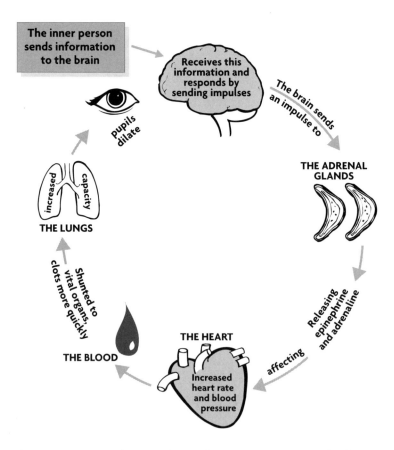

When we perceive danger, this information is sent to the brain, and a sequence of physiological events occurs.

WHEN FEAR DOESN'T SEEM LIKE SUCH A GOOD GIFT

If you are plagued by out-of-control or irrational fears, then your body's response mechanisms may seem more like your enemy than an ally. Why is it that sometimes fear is good, while at other times it can be a problem?

God gave your body the ability to respond to *real* danger. The problem, of course, is that your body (which includes your brain) can't differentiate between real and imagined danger. It doesn't know the difference between a real train and one that exists only in your mind. So if your mind telegraphs news of danger to your brain, your brain will respond the way it was created to. When fear gets out of hand, the problem is not with your brain; it's with the imaginations of the mind that are spawning your brain's responses.

We often struggle with anxiety because we use our God-given ability to imagine a situation in our heart in the wrong way. As C. H. Spurgeon (1834–1892) once preached to his congregation:

> Many of God's people are constantly under apprehensions of calamities which will never occur to them, and they suffer far more in merely dreading them than they would have to endure if they actually came upon them. In their imagination, there are rivers in their way, and they are anxious to know how they shall wade through them, or swim across them. There are no such rivers in existence, but they are agitated and distressed about them. . . . They stab themselves with imaginary daggers, they starve themselves in imaginary famines, and even bury themselves in imaginary graves. *Such strange creatures are we that we probably smart more under blows which never fall upon us than we do under those which do actually come.* The rod of God does not smite us as sharply as the rod of our own imagination does; our groundless fears are our chief tormentors.[1]

HOW OUR BODY RESPONDS
TO FEARFUL IMAGINATIONS

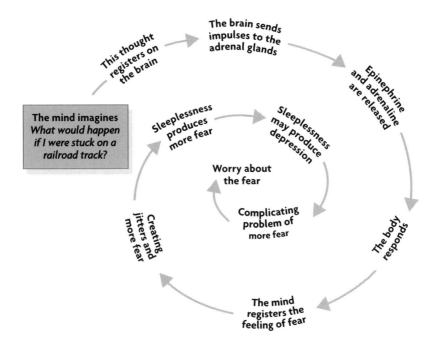

WHEN FEAR BECOMES HABITUAL

Some people are prone to attacks of fear that are characterized by frightening physical responses. These are usually called panic attacks. The physical responses associated with a panic attack can include a rapid heartbeat, fast breathing, and a feeling of impending doom. What's even more frightening is that these physical changes seem to come out of the blue. If you suffer panic attacks, the most disconcerting part of the problem is that you feel like you are out of control. How can you control the panic when you don't even know what's causing it?

Although you're probably not aware of it, your panic began (and continues) because you've entertained fearful thoughts over and over until they've become habitual. God gave us the wonderful ability to make habits, and this ability extends to our thought life. When we repeatedly think about fearful events that might happen, it doesn't take long for us to make a habit of those thoughts. Then, very soon, they'll so permeate our mind that we don't have to intentionally think them—they're just there, in the background, all the time.

The power of habitual thinking can be so strong in some people that eventually, the instant a thought is produced in their imagination, they'll register a visceral feeling of discomfort. Why does this happen? Because of the plasticity or mutability of the brain. Over time, new neural pathways can be created by a habit of thought so that even the slightest suggestion of a frightening imagination can instantaneously produce a rapid heartbeat or upset stomach. For some people, this physical reaction can be overwhelming in its intensity. It occurs quickly and without thoughtful awareness on our part, so that the experience of panic attacks seems very mysterious and overwhelming and we're likely to assume something is happening to our body that has nothing to do with what we were just thinking. But in reality, we have simply practiced this fearful thought long enough that we react physically in an out-of-control way every time it arises.

WHEN IT'S OUR BODY THAT MAKES US FEEL PANICKY

On the other hand, physical symptoms associated with the fight-or-flight state can produce panic *apart* from fearful thoughts. In chapter 2 we mentioned that the heart influences the body, and the body in turn influences the heart. In the case of panic, anxiety can produce physical symptoms such as a rapid heartbeat or a sensation of tightness in the chest; but we also know that a rapid heartbeat (caused by side effects of medicine or actual disease) can also *produce* anxiety. For instance, those with asthma may experience anxiety when they are short of breath, or those taking certain medications can experience a rapid heartbeat caused by their medicine. When your body signals that something is wrong, your mind will probably respond with anxious thoughts. Also, in rare cases, some people produce an inappropriate release of adrenaline, resulting in their bodies being in a fight-or-flight condition continually.

Because these conditions are physiological in origin, you'll need to see your doctor if you've begun having panic attacks, just to ensure that you are not experiencing these feelings because of some undiagnosed disease. Although most panic attacks are related to anxiety, a very small number of women get these frightening physical symptoms because of heart, lung, or adrenal gland disease, or because of a medicine side effect. A visit with your doctor will put your concerns about this to rest.

Because the majority of women who struggle with panic don't have a physical problem, we'll delve more deeply now into what the Bible has to say about our fearful thoughts.

These Imaginations Are Hard to Bear

As Spurgeon wisely noted, the blows that we experience only in our imagination are far worse than any tragedies that actually do come upon us. Why? Because, as His child, God has promised to protect you from trials that are too difficult for you (1 Corinthians 10:13), and He has promised to be with you in any trial that He does allow:

> When you pass through the waters, I will be with you; and through the rivers, they will not overflow you. When you walk through the fire, you will not be scorched, nor will the flame burn you. For I am the Lord your God, the Holy One of Israel, your Savior. . . . Since you are precious in My sight, since you are honored and I love you. . . . Do not fear, for I am with you. (Isaiah 43:2–5; see also Hebrews 13:5–6)

Although it's true God protects us from trials that would be too difficult for us to bear, and although He's promised to walk through every fire with us, He hasn't promised to shower us with grace to endure trials that exist only in our mind. No, He's provided His Word to tell us what parameters to build around our thought life so that we aren't terrorized by imaginary specters of impending doom. When we spend our days in needless worry and anxiety, we're taking all the grace He's given us for each day's activities and wasting it on trials that aren't even here yet or never will be.

When our mind isn't tethered to the truth of Scripture, instead of being a good gift, fear becomes a dreaded enemy. Thankfully, Scripture is powerful enough to help you understand your thoughts (Hebrews 4:12), and it teaches you the kinds of thoughts God commands you to think.

FEAR AND YOUR HEART

Reading the Treasure Map of Your Heart

Jesus Christ, who knows the thoughts of every person's heart (John 2:24–25), knows how we all struggle with our fears and anxieties. In the Sermon on the Mount, He spent a great deal of time counseling His followers on this very topic. Jesus begins this sweet discourse on fear and worry by talking about treasures:

> Do not store up for yourselves treasures on earth, where moth and rust destroy, and where thieves break in and steal. But store up for yourselves treasures in heaven, where neither moth nor rust destroys, and where thieves do not break in or steal; for where your treasure is, there your heart will be also. (Matthew 6:19–21)

The root of our worry and fear is often this: the love of earthly treasure. So as we seek to find God's peace from our troubling emotions, we have to begin by looking into our hearts to see what's glittering there.

An example of this kind of earthly treasure might be an excessive delight in feeling loved. If, in your heart, there is a great desire for others to love you, you'll worry about losing that love. This might play out in your life by worrying incessantly about what others think of you. You'll be afraid to let others into your heart and life and you'll build defenses to keep them out; you might even act cold or distant from others (even though you want their love) because you're afraid they might reject you. This can lead you once again to worrying about how others view you—keeping you trapped in a constant cycle of anxiety and desire.

In contrast to a common misconception, this kind of self-protective behavior doesn't stem from low self-esteem. Rather, it stems from the fact that you have earthly passions that are ruling your heart. Fear and worry are just indications that there is treasure buried nearby. You can begin to uncover these hidden treasures by asking yourself:

- *What do I most commonly worry about losing?*
- *What makes me most happy when I think I've gained it?*

An important step to overcoming your worries, fears, panics, and even your compulsive thoughts is to pinpoint what you love most. For instance, the thought of doing well on a test can be so pleasurable that it breeds terror at the imagination of failure. Some women are so demanding of themselves they think that if they don't do things perfectly, they have not done well at all. Others look at success as the pathway to being loved. Of course, when you're ruled by these extreme emotions, your thinking will be clouded and you'll continually second-guess yourself, resulting in doing poorly and reinforcing fear cycles.

HOW TREASURING PERFECTIONISM BREEDS FEAR

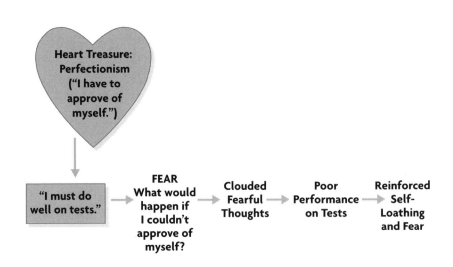

When you habitually embrace earthly treasures, you'll find your life is open to being filled with every permutation of fear, beginning with a simple garden variety of worry all the way to obsessive-compulsive disorder.

THE FEAR CONTINUUM

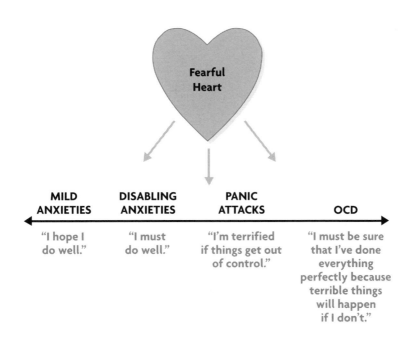

MILD ANXIETIES	DISABLING ANXIETIES	PANIC ATTACKS	OCD
"I hope I do well."	"I must do well."	"I'm terrified if things get out of control."	"I must be sure that I've done everything perfectly because terrible things will happen if I don't."

The Treasure Transfer

Jesus' answer to this distressing cycle is liberating. He simply asks us to value heavenly things. When you value God, His kingdom, His love, His approval, all the other loves that tug on your heart are drained of their power to enslave. You see, as Matthew Henry (1662–1714) says, "Our hearts follow our treasure like the sunflower follows the sun."[2]

HOW TREASURING
THE LORD BRINGS PEACE

Heart Treasure:
Pleasing God
by Faith

"I want to do my best on tests, for God's glory" (1 Corinthians 10:31).

"I will study hard and pray for God to be glorified, as He designs" (Philippians 4:6–7).

"I will rest in God's sovereign plan for my life *and* this test" (Psalm 115:3).

"Because I've submitted my plan to His will, I can rest in the peace He gives and remember what I have studied" (Philippians 4:7).

"I can be free from self-doubt and recriminations because my life isn't about me, and I'm resting in His hands" (Psalms 115:1; 73:23).

"I am resting in perfect peace in His will, whatever that may be" (Isaiah 26:3).

As we continue to heed Christ's kind counsel to us, we can see that worry (and all its cunning companions) is really a matter of wrong perspectives. You won't have the light you need to see clearly if your mind's eye is focused on distracting loves such as: *I have to do well. People need to approve of me. I want others to think I'm beautiful. I have to feel good or life isn't worth living. I have to be sure nothing bad will ever happen to me.* You'll be like a person with cataracts—you'll know you need to focus on that which is true, but you won't be able to discern your way. The Living Bible paraphrases the next two verses about those kinds of treasures: "If your eye is pure, there will be sunshine in your soul. But if your eye is clouded with evil thoughts and desires, you are in deep spiritual darkness. And oh, how deep that darkness can be!" (Matthew 6:22–23).

If our hearts are captivated by temporal treasures, then there will be darkness in our souls. You'll be able to feel this darkness of soul because you'll be filled with needless terrors and unrelenting dread. Of course, the truth is that nothing here on this earth is guaranteed. God hasn't promised to always protect your treasure from capture or decay, so if you spend your life trying to do that, you'll find yourself filled with terrors because we all know that we simply can't control the future. In fact, we can't even control the present.

OBSESSIVE-COMPULSIVE DISORDER AND SELF-INJURY

If you struggle with anxiety, you may have developed a habit of performing certain behaviors that make you feel more in control over the things that make you anxious. This behavior pattern is sometimes known as obsessive-compulsive disorder (OCD). Heart attitudes in people who struggle with these habits can include a desire for certainty or control, and a desire to do things perfectly. A person who wants to know what is going to happen, be in charge of it, and always do it perfectly will feel anxious most of the time because none of us can consistently achieve a standard such as this. Even though most of us know perfection is an impossible goal, we will pursue it just the same.

We often develop a habit of checking things over and over to make sure they have been done right. Or we may develop a standard of cleanliness or order that is so strict that we find ourselves upset if it is disturbed in the slightest way. This should make us feel safer, right? But at this point the trap springs shut. The very things that we started doing because they made us feel in control begin to *control us*. When we practice these habits we feel worse, but not practicing them makes us feel even worse yet![3]

HOW THE DESIRE FOR
CONTROL BREEDS SLAVERY

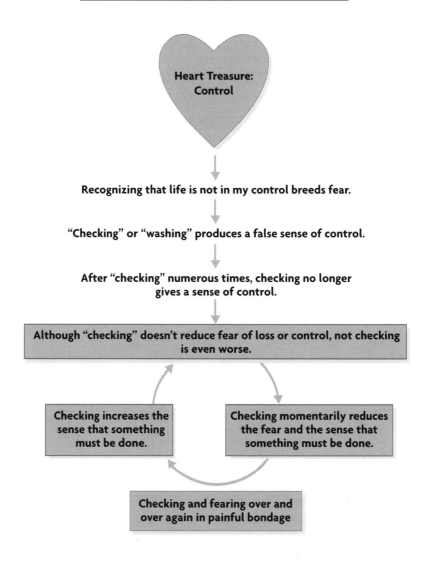

Women who have developed self-injurious habits often have similar heart attitudes, such as perfectionism or the desire to be in control. If you've found it difficult to speak openly about your worries (for whatever reason), you might also have found that acting on them brings you a sense of comfort or release. The pain that you inflict on yourself is, after all, more manageable than the pain that is outside of your control. If your worries produce a feeling of unbearable tension inside you and you aren't able to talk about them, you may find yourself tempted to do anything, even hurt yourself, to relieve yourself of it. Whether the self-injury includes skin picking, hair pulling (trichotillomania), cutting, the restrictive dieting of anorexia, or the binge-and-purge cycle of bulimia, these habits do seem to ease anxiety *temporarily*. But before long the anxiety returns, and the desire to act on it begins to build again.[4]

Neither OCD behaviors nor self-injury can produce lasting peace in those who practice them. Those who have been performing these behaviors for a long time feel trapped and compelled to repeat them for even temporary relief. In a sense they have an addiction. The drive to do something that makes them feel better in the short-term produces worse feelings in the long-term.

HOW THE DESIRE FOR PERFECTION
AND CONTROL BREEDS SLAVERY

Heart Treasures:
Self-perfection
Control

I recognize that life is out of control and I'm not perfect.

The desire and pressure to be perfect builds and builds
with every attempt and failure.

If I inflict pain on myself, it distracts me from the pain of my failure.

I feel some pleasure in the pain, but I also feel guilty and imperfect over having
injured myself, and I feel pressure to escape my guilt through pain again.

I continue to fail, I'm not getting perfection, and I'm not changing.

I injure myself and feel
momentary relief, but then
guilt and self-
abhorrence crowd in.

My guilt and sense of failure
grow so I want to distract
my thoughts through pain.

FREEDOM FROM ENSLAVING FEARS

The only hope we have of finding liberty from our enslaving fears is to focus our love on God and rest in His promise to be with us and keep us. Jesus said it plainly: "You cannot serve God and wealth"

(Matthew 6:24). Although it's true He was speaking of the folly of loving money, let's not assume that's all He meant. He was talking about treasure again—you can't love and devote yourself to your treasure and think that you can love and devote yourself to God at the same time. If you're filled with any of the myriad fears or anxieties we've mentioned in this chapter, it's because you're trying to divide your heart, and that's impossible to do.

So it's when you feel that panic arising, when you toss and turn all night from worry, or when you're tempted to go check the light switch for the tenth time, that God is graciously informing you that your heart is following the wrong sun. Here's what your heart or mind's eye needs to focus on:

> I say to you, do not be worried about your life, as to what you will eat or what you will drink; nor for your body, as to what you will put on. Is not life more than food, and the body more than clothing? Look at the birds of the air, that they do not sow, nor reap nor gather into barns, and yet your heavenly Father feeds them. Are you not worth much more than they? And who of you by being worried can add a single hour to his life? And why are you worried about clothing? Observe how the lilies of the field grow; they do not toil nor do they spin, yet I say to you that not even Solomon in all his glory clothed himself like one of these. But if God so clothes the grass of the field, which is alive today and tomorrow is thrown into the furnace, will He not much more clothe you? You of little faith! Do not worry then, saying, "What will we eat?" or "What will we drink?" or "What will we wear for clothing?" For the Gentiles eagerly seek all these things; for your heavenly Father knows that you need all these things. But seek first His kingdom and His righteousness, and all these things will be added to you. (Matthew 6:25–33)

We're not to love or focus our lives on self-promotion, self-protection, self-gratification, or self-indulgence. Rather, as Jesus says, "Don't worry! Your life is far more than being sure people respect you or assuring yourself that you're completely safe. It's more than making sure you'll always have everything you need." The One who alone knows our hearts as they really are has one very powerful word of advice: Your heavenly Father is aware and able to provide everything you really need. Here are some practical ways this kind of knowledge might help you:

Worrisome Thought	Faithful Thought	Scriptural Truth	Focusing on the Kingdom and Righteous Living
What will happen if my husband loses his job?	God is able to provide for me. He knows what I need, and He's promised to care for me.	Matthew 6:25–33; Philippians 4:19; Psalm 23	Pray for my husband; be thankful for what God has provided for me today.
How could I have any peace if I fail my test?	God is able to make me successful if that's what's best for me. He knows what I need, and I can trust Him.	Psalm 75: 6–7; Daniel 5:18	Study a reasonable amount of time. Pray that God will help me. Get good rest before the test.
What if my best friend deserts me?	When I'm focused on being loved, I'm not focused on loving others. God knows what I need, and He's promised that He'd never leave or forsake me.	Matthew 22:39; Philippians 2:3–11; Hebrews 13:5–6	Look for opportunities to serve my friend and share her with others for their benefit.
What if I get sick from someone else's germs?	Every molecule in all creation is under God's sovereign rule. If God allows sickness into my life, it will ultimately be for my good and His glory. He knows what I need.	Matthew 6:26; Daniel 4:35; Job 23:13; Psalm 115:3	Try to be reasonably healthy and look for opportunities to serve the sick.
What if I say something blasphemous or hurt someone?	God knows your heart! He didn't send His Son to die for perfect people, but rather for sinners who need His help. If you unwillingly think a wicked thought or say something that seems blasphemous, His forgiveness can reach even to you. Remember, He forgave people who crucified His Son.	Mark 2:17; Psalm 139:4; 1 John 1:9	Rather than focusing on what I might say, I'll focus on what I should say. I will practice speech that is honoring and gentle. If I do say something unkind or even blasphemous, I'll ask God to forgive me and move on.
What if I embarrass myself by passing out or vomiting in public?	If I am embarrassed because I'm seeking to obey God, I can rejoice that I'm being a fool for Him; being embarrassed because I'm obedient is better than being embarrassed because I'm being disobedient and faithless. God knows what I need.	1 Corinthians 3:18; 2 Corinthians 11:16; 2 Samuel 6:20–22; 1 John 4:18	I must love God and others enough to risk being thought foolish.

As you look over the verses in the chart, can you see how practical and freeing the Lord's advice is? Over and over again He reminds our timid hearts, "Your Father knows what you need. You're of value to Me, and when you forget that truth, you'll live like an unbeliever—always filled with worries and fears. Focus on obeying Me, and *everything* you need will be given to you!"

You've Got Enough to Handle Today

The Lord finished His discourse on needless fears by stating, "Do not worry about tomorrow; for tomorrow will care for itself. Each day has enough trouble of its own" (Matthew 6:34).

Although we shouldn't live our lives pragmatically, trying to seek out "whatever works," we can't ignore the pragmatic nature of Christ's words. In essence He said, "Live in the moment right now; seek to be faithful and love Me and others right now, and don't be carried away by what might happen tomorrow. After all, I've given you the grace you need for today only, and when tomorrow comes—if it does!—I'll give you the grace you need then."

Now that we've looked at what our Lord taught about fears and worry, let's take a quick journey into the thoughts of the apostle Paul on the subject.

PAUL'S ADVICE ABOUT FEAR

Be Anxious for Nothing

Paul's advice about fears and worries is similar to that of Jesus. And it's encouraging to know that Paul was weak and sinful just like us. Here is his counsel:

> The Lord is near. Be anxious for nothing, but in everything by prayer and supplication with thanksgiving let your requests be made known to God. And the peace of God, which surpasses all comprehension, will guard your hearts and your minds in Christ Jesus. (Philippians 4:5–7)

First, Paul reminds us that "the Lord is near." Why does he start here? Why doesn't he just tell us not to worry? Because the one truth we need to remember (and keep remembering) is that our Savior is near to us. That's similar to the Lord's counsel about your heavenly Father knowing what you need. He's here—that's what we need to know.

Paul then tells his readers not to be anxious about anything—just as Jesus did. "Just don't do it!" they say. In making this imperative command, Paul kicks the importance of our discussion up into another category. He's saying that worry and anxiety aren't just trivial problems. He's calling them sin. Again, please don't despair—recognizing that our emotional pain is sin is actually great news. You see, Jesus Christ didn't die to free us from our *uncomfortable habits*. No, He died to free us from *sin*. He paid the price for every ounce of worry and fear in each of our lives, and He broke the power that worry (and all our sin) has in our lives. Although it might feel like we're shackled to our enslaving habits, the Bible teaches that we are, in fact, free: "Knowing this, that our old self was crucified with Him, in order that our body of sin might be done away with, so that we would no longer be slaves to sin" (Romans 6:6).

If you've identified with the death, burial, and resurrection of Jesus Christ, then this is the truth: You're free from your bondage to sin. Your habitual fears and anxieties might seem like they'll never let you go, but that's not the truth. The truth is that the Lord has set you free.

Pray with Thanksgiving About Everything

Paul then continues his counsel by telling us what to do with our concerns: We're to pray with thanksgiving. Paul doesn't tell us to pretend that nothing is wrong in our lives. No, he knows that as long as we live here in this sin-cursed world, we'll have problems. When we recognize that a worry, fear, or obsession seems to be overpowering us, we're to bring it to our heavenly Father, who already knows what we need (but wants us to ask).

Here's how you can intentionally follow the Lord in this: In the chart below, we've made a place for you to list your concerns. Put a check mark next to those that aren't in your power or your responsibility to do anything about. These are the concerns you'll need to pray about and *leave* in the hands of God. Put an arrow next to those you have responsibility for and make another list (in order of importance) of these tasks you need to complete. Don't forget to pray about these as well.[5]

My Worries	✓ or →	My Responsibilities
		1.
		2.
		3.
		4.
		5.
		6.
		7.
		8.

Once you've listed and prayed about your concerns, you'll want to continue to follow Paul's advice by spending time being thankful. Pondering all the ways that God has been faithful in the past and remembering His goodness to you when you knew you didn't deserve it will certainly encourage your faith and give you the courage to carry on. Stop now and think: *What am I most thankful for?* Your list might include God's benefits to you, such as the gift of salvation or His Word or His grace, or it might also consist of your earthly blessings. Has He been faithful to preserve and protect you so far? How has He used your failures for your good? What have you learned about suffering through them?

Now that you've prayed and thought about the Lord's kindness to you, look over the list of concerns and start working on the first one. Don't worry about whether you'll be able to finish it right away or perfectly—just begin to plug away at it in faith. "Lord, I'm beginning this for You and I'm trusting that You'll help me finish it for You. I know You're with me, and I thank You for Your Word," you might pray.

Once you've done this you'll discover the most pleasing result: The peace of God, something we'll never understand, will begin to guard your heart and your mind. When you struggle with any kind of emotional pain, pray. Then tell yourself, *I've prayed about this, and I know that my Father heard me. I'm no longer going to allow myself to become distressed over a matter I've left in God's hands.*

Control Your Thoughts

The next counsel Paul gives us is to control our thoughts. In fact, he gives us a grid whereby we can check to see if our thoughts are worthy to be entertained:

> Finally, brethren, whatever is true, whatever is honorable, whatever is right, whatever is pure, whatever is lovely, whatever is of good repute, if there is any excellence and if anything worthy of praise, dwell on these things. The things you have learned and received and heard and seen in me, practice these things, and the God of peace will be with you. (Philippians 4:8–9)

Paul wants each of us to learn, by God's grace, to control our thoughts and imaginations. He tells us there are eight filters through which we should judge our thoughts:

Thought Filter	Ask Yourself:
True	Is what I'm thinking *true* about God, particularly His fatherly care for me?
Honorable	Do my thoughts honor God? Do they reflect the knowledge that He is wonderful, kind, loving, wise, and powerful?
Right	Are my thoughts holy, righteous, or just? Are they the kind the Lord Himself would think?
Pure	Do my thoughts cast doubt on God's goodness or the truth of His promises? Do they elevate my own importance or desires?
Lovely	Do my thoughts flow from a heart filled with tenderness and affection for the Lord? Would my thoughts bring Him pleasure?
Of Good Repute	Are my thoughts grounded in faith? Do they exalt God's reputation?
Excellent	Do my thoughts cause me to be more fearful, or do they fill my heart with courage and strong commitment to virtuous living?
Praiseworthy	Would the Lord commend my thoughts? Would they elevate His name or bring Him glory?

Whenever a fearful thought comes into your mind, you can stop it and ask yourself, *Is this thought true? Honorable? Right? Pure? Lovely? Of good repute? Excellent? Praiseworthy? If not, then I should not dwell on it!*

Paul's final advice to us is to practice these disciplines over and over again—until they become second nature. This may prove difficult. We all tend to be pretty good at starting things, and not as great at staying consistent with them. Practice also means that we won't get it right the first time around. We'll have to work hard to control our anxious thoughts, especially when it seems like we're losing the battle. But we can rest in the knowledge that God is working with us in this and that God's peace will be in us.

THE RIGHT KIND OF FEAR

There are two types of fear mentioned in Scripture. There is the fear that God has commanded us to resist, and there's the fear of Him that He commands. The fear that He's commanded is not a slavish, cringing type that frightens us into hiding from Him. No, it's more like a "reverent submission that leads to obedience. . . . Like terror, it includes a clear-eyed knowledge of God's justice and His anger against sin. But this worship-fear also knows God's great forgiveness, mercy, and love."[6]

The right kind of fear is a weapon powerful enough to overcome the wrong kinds of fear. When you're tempted to stay in and not go to a church gathering because you're afraid someone might think, do, or say something about you or to you, the healthy fear of God will come to your rescue. You can say to yourself, *It may be that when I get to church something bad might happen, and I'm afraid of that. But I know that the only motive that's worth my love and service is worship of the God whom I love, and since He's commanded me to meet regularly with other believers, I'm going to obey Him. If something bad happens there, then I'll just trust that the Lord will use it in my life for my good. Like Shadrach, Meshach, and Abednego* [Daniel 3:19], *I may have to die for my obedience right now, but I refuse to bow down at the altar of my feelings anymore!*

Then, with those thoughts in mind, you'll be able to obey the Lord, and you'll find His peace comforting your heart and the strength of your fears subsiding. Of this you can be certain.

CAST YOUR CARE UPON HIM

As this chapter draws to a close, let's look again at the verse that started the chapter: "Humble yourselves under the mighty hand of God, that He may exalt you at the proper time, casting all your anxiety on Him, because He cares for you" (1 Peter 5:6–7).

Peter's counsel to the anxious is simple: Be humble, trust His timing, and cast all your anxiety on Him. Why? Because He cares for you. Peter tells us that we need to be humble because our fear is rooted in our misplaced pride and trust. Do we really believe that if we dwell long enough on a problem or try hard enough to deal with it, we ourselves will be able to control our circumstances or the future? No amount of worry can change the outcome of anything.

Only God has control of the world and knows the future, and we're far better off leaving our concerns in His hands than keeping them in ours.

Right now the Lord is calling each of us to turn from our proud self-trust and put all of our cares and anxieties on Him. Are you ready to be done with your false hopes? If so, take time now to prayerfully complete the exercises below, and ask the Lord to renew you by His Spirit and assure you of His love. And remember: If you're presently on medication for your fears, please *do not* stop taking it without the direction and help of your physician.

GROWING IN YOUR FAITH

1. Have you considered your treasures? What are you terrified of losing (or never getting)? Are you willing to lay all your treasures down at the feet of the one Treasure who is able to bear the weight of all your desire and longing?

2. David prayed, "Search me, O God, and know my heart; try me and know my anxious thoughts; and see if there be any hurtful way in me, and lead me in the everlasting way" (Psalm 139:23–24). Why not pray this prayer now and ask God to search and know your inmost thoughts and worries? And don't stop there. Ask Him to know the "hurtful way" that's residing in your heart, and then to lead you by His gentle hand.

3. If you know your faith needs to grow, begin today to memorize the Scriptures in this chapter. You could begin with 1 Peter 5:6–7, or any part of the passages from Matthew 6 or Philippians 4:6–9.

4. Did you complete the "Concern List" on page 139? If not, would you please do so now? After you've completed this list, write ten items you're thankful for. List them here.

5. Summarize, in four or five sentences, what you learned in this chapter.

Mary Lou's Story

In March 1999, I fell and broke my tibia (one of the two bones between the knee and ankle) in a hot tub accident. The subsequent surgery required the insertion of a plate and pins into the broken bone and a bone graft from my hip. This was followed by eight weeks of no walking and a year of rehabilitation. I experienced a lot of pain and found myself totally dependent upon others.

Just as I was getting back to normal, my mother died unexpectedly. We were very close, and it broke my heart to lose her. Shortly after that I lost my part-time job. This sequence of traumatic events took its toll on me, and I had a hard time staying focused on my responsibilities. I would wander around the house trying to decide what to do, and end up doing nothing. Routine tasks seemed burdensome and overwhelming. At my annual medical checkup, I told the doctor that I was feeling anxious.

The doctor prescribed an antidepressant, which made me feel even more anxious. Over a period of several months I tried twelve different medications and saw ten different doctors. I was told over and over that I could not get well on my own— that I needed these medications to "balance the chemicals in my brain." Some medications made me sick to the point of vomiting. I couldn't stay home alone, my heart pounded, I'd wake up late at night shaking and soaked in sweat, and I felt like I was going crazy.

Eventually I met with a Christian psychologist. His style of counseling was not helpful; it focused on self and dwelling on the past. It also minimized God, the biblical view of sin, and personal responsibility. I then began seeing a biblical counselor who showed me what God's Word said about my problems. This counselor emphasized that my life was not about me, but about glorifying God no matter what my circumstances.

Through biblical counseling I learned that the kinds of worries, anxieties, and depressed thoughts I was having were sinful. I had always thought worry and fear were just a part of who I was, and didn't realize I could change my thought patterns. I learned that our thoughts affect how we feel, and that we are to turn away from wrong thoughts and replace them with God's truth.

During my struggles I often asked God, Why are You allowing this to happen? Why don't You take away this anxiety? *Later I learned that instead of asking God why, I should trust His wisdom. When we don't trust God, we doubt His sovereignty and goodness.*

The most valuable lesson I learned was to memorize Scripture. I had always avoided doing this because I'm not good at it. But learning verses that I could meditate upon when my thoughts were headed down the wrong path helped me to be able to focus on God's truths and turn around my thoughts.

Eventually I did recover and stop my medications. I sought help from a naturopathic doctor because my body had gone through so much from the multiple medications. Vitamins, B-complex shots, and mineral IVs helped restore my health. I still have a tendency toward worry and fear, but I am alert to such emotions now and can turn away from them much more quickly. I know God is sufficient for me, and I know I can trust Him with every detail of my life—even when it hurts.

SEVEN

UNDERSTANDING YOUR OUT-OF-CONTROL MOODS

THE FRUIT OF THE SPIRIT IS LOVE, JOY, PEACE,
PATIENCE, KINDNESS, GOODNESS, FAITHFULNESS,
GENTLENESS, SELF-CONTROL.

Galatians 5:22–23

Hormonal hostage!
I'm out of estrogen and I have a gun!
Just hand over the chocolate and nobody gets hurt!

WE'VE ALL SEEN the bumper stickers, and they make us laugh. Who among women hasn't found herself in the grip of a strange monthly madness? Who hasn't behaved in ways she wouldn't normally when under stress? More frighteningly, who hasn't at one time or another felt totally mastered by anger, fear, irritability, or worse, by an irresistible impulse?

But maybe you have a bigger problem than occasional episodes of unpleasant behavior. Perhaps it's become normal for you to feel as if you're forced to do whatever your emotions dictate. Or you may be losing the battle against substance abuse, and as you are drawn into more drinking or drugs, you find yourself becoming more unpredictable. You may have seen a doctor who told you that you have premenstrual dysphoric disorder or bipolar disorder. Does this mean that you have a disease, and that you will be like this for the rest of your life?

In this chapter we are going to apply what we learned in the first section of this book to the specific problem of mood swings. We'll consider what contribution our bodies may make to our mood, and we'll also look at how trouble of the heart can produce patterns of instability in our lives.

WHERE DID THAT COME FROM?

We sometimes find ourselves saying, "I can't believe I just did that! Where did that come from?" Then we remember that the Bible tells us exactly where our words and behaviors come from: our hearts. When we are irritable at that time of the month, we can't tell ourselves that our hormones made us do it (no matter how much we may want to!). And although our physical condition is not the actual source of our behavior, remember from chapter 2 that it *can* influence our heart. Let's begin our study of mood swings by looking at the common physical challenges that accompany PMS, pregnancy, and menopause.

HORMONES AND EMOTIONS

Many women are more emotional or irritable before the onset of their period. Some have painful cramping, water retention, headaches, and bodily aches. Some experience cravings for salt or sugar that, if indulged, may worsen how they feel. When we're uncomfortable we're more likely to be crabby, and we may also find ourselves bothered by things that would not upset us if we were feeling better.

It's also possible that changing hormonal levels during the premenstrual stage may have a more direct effect on our emotional responses. Some women find they are especially passionate around the time they ovulate. Before their periods, some women struggle with feeling fat or ugly, whereas they are not preoccupied with their appearance at any other time of the month. Others find depression or anxiety troubles them before their periods, but they are quite stable the rest of the month.

Why do these things happen? There is much that doctors don't understand about the interaction between female hormones and other organs of our bodies. For instance, why can diseases such as asthma, migraines, allergies, and seizures become worse just before our periods, or with pregnancy? In the same way that these illnesses may be affected by interactions between our hormones and other bodily organs, perhaps our more powerful emotions at some times of the month are linked to similar interactions.

Pregnancy is a state that is definitely linked to changes in emotions. A woman's emotional experience in pregnancy is often colored by how physically challenging it is and by what else is going on in her life. Interestingly, although some women find themselves more emotional during pregnancy, others find that they are more relaxed and placid than usual.

Many women who are beyond their thirties have perimenopausal and menopausal symptoms. The most troubling of these are hot flashes and sleep disturbance. Some of them also have strong emotional ups and downs. Doctors think that the emotional problems may be linked to frequent awakening during hot flashes, which occur more often at night. The resulting sleep deprivation is a well-known cause of crankiness and a tendency to blow small problems out of proportion.

Whatever physical reason there may be for our having a stronger emotional response than usual, this does not change the biblical truth that although our physical state may influence our heart, it does not *cause* our emotional reactions. And so to begin to get our emotional responses under control, we need to look to our heart and ask ourselves what is really going on inside us.

HORMONES AND FEELING IRRITABLE

The physical changes induced by hormones can contribute to irritability, but this doesn't mean that your hormones made you snap at your husband the last time he asked for dinner while you were lying down with a headache at that time of the month. Let's think about what might have been going on in your heart, along with that headache in your body, when your husband came into the room.

What was your first response when you saw him? Maybe you thought, *Oh no, what does he want now? I was just getting relaxed!* When he made his request you may have thought, *Can't he get dinner himself just this once? He knows I get headaches this time of the month!* If you're like us, it's just a quick jump from this thought to, *He's so selfish! He never asks how he can help me!* If you're thinking thoughts like these, are you more likely to respond to him with kindness and love, or with bitter words?

Let's go a little deeper with this example. What might have been the bottom line of the thoughts you were thinking? Perhaps you thought, *My headache is more important than his stupid dinner!* If so, your angry words came as a predictable result of a heart attitude that said that you are more important than your husband.

When we are feeling like this, we may think that we have the right to be upset with someone who has failed to consider our needs. But the Bible tells us that we shouldn't be concentrating on our needs. According to Jesus, our attitude should be this:

> Whoever would be great among you must be your servant, and whoever would be first among you must be slave of all. For even the Son of Man came not to be served but to serve, and to give his life as a ransom for many. (Mark 10:43–45 ESV; see also Philippians 2:3–4)

Because of our fallen state as humans, this servant attitude doesn't come naturally to us. The Bible says we tend to place our own interests ahead of serving God and others. That's why we can expect to find a core of selfishness at the heart of our angry, impulsive, or irritable response, even when physical issues such as our monthly cycle are involved.

Idols of the Heart

John Calvin once said that our hearts are like idol factories.[1]

What he meant is that, in our hearts, placing other people or things ahead of God comes very naturally. Whatever we consider more important than pleasing God functions as a substitute god, or idol, for us.

One way to try to ferret out whatever idols may be lurking in your heart is to ask yourself the following questions: *What do I think I must have to be happy? What do I think I can't live without?* Your answers may be idols in your life, the things that you want more than you want to please God.[2] If you believe that you should always come first in your husband's eyes, could this attitude be at the heart of your monthly crabbiness? If you value your own personal peace and comfort more than obedience to Christ's command, this may explain why you have difficulty responding with kindness to a request that conflicts with your desire for comfort.

As we learned earlier, any habit of thought will reveal itself in our behavior sooner or later. The emotions we experience before our periods are telling us about our hearts. Then, of course, that which is in our hearts will eventually appear in our behavior, as Jesus said it would (Luke 6:45).

Follow Your Heart?

In chapter 1 we learned that God intends for our feelings to reveal to us what's happening in our hearts. Our feelings should only *inform* us, not *lead* us. You may agree this is true, but you may still find it hard to resist the desire to make choices based upon your feelings. Perhaps as a child you were not taught how to handle your feelings in a self-controlled manner. Your parents may have let their emotions lead them, and this way of life may feel as natural as breathing to you. Maybe you never even considered the possibility of listening to your emotions without following them until you began reading this book. After all, aren't books and movies full of stories of people who followed their hearts . . . and lived happily ever after?

We've come to think our feelings can tell us what is right and true. Consider the messages the world tells us: *Let conscience be your guide. If it feels right, it must be okay. Trust your feelings.*

But the Bible tells us that even what seems the most normal and natural to us may be wrong. Hear Proverbs 14:12: "There is a way which seems right to a man, but its end is the way of death." We are commanded to "put to death therefore what is earthly [that is, what comes naturally] in you" (Colossians 3:5 ESV). If we keep doing the wrong things that come so naturally to us, we will become spiritually weak. Instead, by the Holy Spirit's power, we need to put on the new self (Ephesians 4:24; Colossians 3:9–11), a new set of habit patterns that are based upon the commands of God's Word. We will discuss the "putting on" of new habit patterns in more detail in chapter 9.

As Christians, we need to learn to be guided by Scripture rather than our feelings. We will never gain control of our unruly emotions until we choose to begin dealing with them in a different way. The rest of this chapter will give you tools that can help you change your habits. Why don't you take a moment to ask God to help you understand how to follow His truth instead of your feelings?

HABIT OR DISEASE?

If you struggle on a daily basis with emotions that seem uncontrollable, you may have been told you suffer from the disease of manic depression or bipolar disorder. But based on our experience, we believe many women who have been diagnosed with bipolar disorder actually have a problem with habitually following their unstable emotions and don't have a disease. If that's true for you, then it's good news, because habits can be changed, while diseases often can't.

It is true there is an agitated psychotic state called *mania*. For information on this very serious problem, please turn to chapter 8, which deals with psychotic conditions in detail. But most women who have been diagnosed with bipolar disorder have never had a manic psychosis. Let's try to understand why this has occurred.

Until fairly recently, bipolar disorder was believed to be a rare condition. But a "new condition," Bipolar Disorder II, became popular about twenty years ago. It is now diagnosed frequently, especially in women. Bipolar II, as it is often called, is characterized by an unstable mood that does not meet the diagnostic criteria for classic manic depression (also called Bipolar I). How was this "new condition" discovered? Doctors began giving mood-stabilizing medicines to people with unstable emotions. Nearly all of them had prior diagnoses of depression and were already receiving antidepressants. When they began to feel worse on these medications, a new diagnosis was made, and a second drug was prescribed to them.

Mood instability, and even mania, are known antidepressant side effects. We wonder how much of the increase in Bipolar II diagnoses may be attributable to the increase in prescriptions for antidepressants. Can you see how "poop-out" or a manic side effect could lead to therapeutic tail-chasing and a diagnosis of Bipolar II? Bill and Laura both became unstable after they began to take antidepressants for simple depression. Their instability later led to serious suicidal thoughts for both of them.

If you have been diagnosed with bipolar disorder and have never been psychotic, we want to give you hope that you can break the cycle of unstable moods. Many women with this diagnosis have learned to cope with their emotions and have been able to stop taking the medicines prescribed to people with such conditions. In Laura's case, this was literally lifesaving. By contrast, Bill continued to rely upon his medicine. When his hope that his medications would help him feel better ended, he also ended his life.

We understand that your mood swings seem to come from outside of you like an irresistible force. But the Bible tells us that what we think in our hearts drives how we feel. Since this is true, we can have great hope that changing our thoughts and responses can help make us more stable.

UNDERSTANDING THE MOOD-SWING CYCLE

Discouragement and Mood Swings

Is there another way to understand unstable moods besides viewing them as a disease that has no connection to your thoughts and choices? We believe it is helpful to view the mood-swing process as a cycle in which our responses to stress produce emotions that make us feel worse. This feeling worse, in turn, produces more emotions, which make us feel even worse. This cycle can continue until our emotions are totally out of control. Let us explain how this works.

Because you are reading this book, we suspect you are serious about your Christian walk. You want to please God, and you are trying to battle wrong impulses. If these things weren't true about you, we imagine you would have stopped reading this book before now.

But your desire to do good, and the unhappiness you feel when you fall short, may be at the core of some of your struggles with your emotions. Maybe you have a temper and work hard to keep it under control. Or maybe you are prone to fear, and you try not to panic when a person or circumstance disturbs you. And at the times when you do lash out or panic, you feel bad because you've blown it.

You may have a hard time forgiving yourself and may question how God could love someone who fails as often as you do. You may have even resorted to punishing yourself in hopes that this will motivate you to do better in the future. But the sad truth is that mere human resolve never works. The end result of trying to change in our own power is depression and despair.

The Bible tells us we are soldiers in a war against the sin in our hearts (2 Corinthians 10:3–5). And when we're continually discouraged and depressed, we become easy prey for Satan's temptations. With each failure, we become more depressed, which makes us more vulnerable to temptation the next time around. As we give in to temptation again and again, we may find that it becomes harder to resist.

THE MOOD-SWING CYCLE

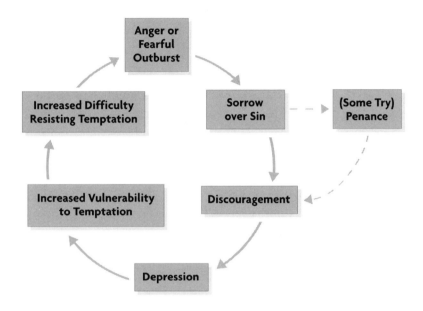

Perfectionism and Mood Swings

Here's another example of how a mood-swing cycle can trap us. Tasha is a good artist. She is detail oriented—she wants everything to be just right. It doesn't matter to Tasha whether her project is major or minor.

Imagine with us that Tasha's daughter, Susan, has a kindergarten play that starts in half an hour. Susan may desperately need her mother to be gentle, calm, and reassuring as she gets ready. But if Tasha suddenly decides that Susan's costume (handmade by Tasha) lacks some crucial detail, she may end up screaming at her daughter while trying to get the costume "just right" and still arrive at the play on time. Or perhaps she will manage to control her frustration, but Susan will end up hysterical or cowering in fear because she can't handle the tension she senses.

Either way, Tasha will fail to lovingly nurture Susan because she "majors on the minors." In the words of Jesus, this is "straining out a gnat and swallowing a camel" (Matthew 23:24 ESV). A habit of responding like this causes those whom we love to suffer on account of our insistence that everything be perfect.

Do you see yourself in Tasha? Perhaps you want to do things as well as you can, yet you tend to become obsessed to the point where it affects how you act and treat others. Maybe you've made a habit of placing projects ahead of the important people in your life. If so, you may live in constant turmoil because you alternate between "project frenzy" and the despair that sets in afterward when you fail to achieve your goal or you hurt loved ones along the way.

But our despair doesn't always motivate us to handle ourselves differently the next time. Sometimes we become so discouraged and we think that our performance was so unsatisfactory (or that we were so cruel to our loved ones) that we redouble our efforts to be more perfect the next time around. And so the cycle continues.

A MOOD-SWING CYCLE
FUELED BY PERFECTIONISM

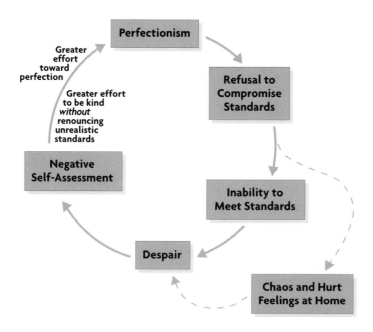

Wrong Emotions and Mood Swings

Any emotion that elicits a sinful response from us can initiate a mood-swing cycle. Since the attitudes of our hearts drive our emotions, any attitude that is based upon wanting something more than we want to please God can be at the heart of these mood swings.

If you find yourself letting your emotions take you down a path you don't want to tread, you are not alone. The apostle Paul described his battle in this way:

> I do not understand my own actions. For I do not do what I want, but I do the very thing I hate. . . . So now it is no longer I who do it, but sin that dwells within me. . . . For I have the desire to do what is right, but not the ability to carry it out. For I do not do the good I want, but the evil I do not want is what I keep on doing. Now if I do what I do not want, it is no longer I who do it, but sin that dwells within me. . . . Wretched man that I am! Who will deliver me from this body of death? (Romans 7:15, 17–20, 24 ESV)

Like us, Paul struggled with a desire to please God and a desire to give in to his human flesh. The Bible tells us that we were born with this natural tendency toward sin (Romans 7:14). While it's true that as Christians we were given a new heart that loves God and wants to obey Him, our new hearts continue to be influenced by what Paul called "sin which dwells within me" (Romans 7:20). We need to battle against sinful tendencies, seeking to put them to death (Romans 8:13). This condition will continue until the day we are raised to eternal life in new bodies (1 Corinthians 15:42–44).

PLEASING YOURSELF OR PLEASING GOD?

You may be thinking, *Well, I believe all that. And I'm trying to do the right thing. So why am I still falling short?* Maybe the problem is that even though you are working as hard as you can on your behavior, you aren't listening to what your emotions are telling you about your underlying heart attitudes or treasures. Is it possible that you're not bearing more of the fruit of the Spirit because your own personal peace, or what other people think about you, is more important to you than pleasing God?

Maybe you want to please God, but when it comes down to choosing between your convenience and God's commands, you find that you don't want to obey God badly enough to say no to your own desires. Or maybe your real goal is to become a nicer person so people will like you rather than to become more holy. If your desire is focused on you rather than God, then you will feel ashamed of your failure *(What will people think?)* rather than sorry before God for your sin. If you respond with shame rather than repentance, you will be tempted to despair over your failure rather than being strengthened in your resolve to please God the next time around. As we have seen, such despair can be the start of a mood-swing cycle.

Or perhaps that isn't your problem. On the contrary, you are aware of what your emotions are telling you about what is important to you, and you may be working diligently to place God first in your heart. But when you fall into sin, you respond to your failures with self-condemnation, and this can suck you back into the mood-swing cycle. How can you break free of this destructive pattern?

KEEPING THE HEART

Proverbs 4:23 says, "Keep your heart with all diligence, for out of it spring the issues of life" (NKJV). We have already discussed how our thoughts, feelings, and choices result from our heart attitudes. But have you ever thought about what you could do to *change* your heart attitudes? This verse contains the key to change. It commands us to "keep," or guard, our hearts. Not only that, but it also commands us to give our best effort.

John Flavel (1630–1691) defined keeping the heart as "the diligent and constant use of all holy means to preserve the soul from sin, and maintain its sweet and free communion with God."[3] He described our heart as a fort under siege, with enemies on the outside and traitors on the inside, whose soldiers are commanded to do everything they can to protect it. But Flavel emphasized that although God commands us to keep our heart, we do not have the power to do it on our own.

Because we cannot keep our hearts except by God's power, we must first be regenerated, or born again, and then receive God's daily cleansing and keeping grace. (If you're not sure what this means, see appendix A, "How You Can Know If You're a Christian.") Flavel went on to say, "As long as a heart is not *set right* by grace . . . it is impossible that any external means [such as discipline or punishment] should keep it with God."[4]

When we were born again, we received initial saving grace. Now, as believers, when we fail to behave in a way that honors God, we can repent of our sinful response and ask Him for the power to act differently the next time. If we do this instead of surrendering to despair, we will receive His cleansing from the guilt of our sin and His grace to keep our heart.

Although we can't keep our heart without God's help, we are still instructed in Proverbs 4:23 to give this our best effort. Now, this may seem confusing. If we can't keep our heart apart from God's power, why are we commanded to exert our own effort?

The Bible is full of what we like to call "my part/His part" commands. For example, Philippians 2:12–13 instructs us to "work out *your* own salvation with fear and trembling, for it is *God* who works in you, both to will and to work for His good pleasure" (emphasis added). We are instructed to trust God for the power to do what He commands; then we are to prayerfully step out by faith and *do* it. This is very different from a passive "let go and let God" attitude.

An important aspect of keeping our heart is to actively feed our minds upon the Bible's truths instead of the world's lies. If we are serious about keeping our heart, we will refuse to entertain thoughts that contradict the Bible's teachings about who we are, the source of our problems, and our ability to change. Instead, we'll actively work to correct our wrong perceptions and replace them with scriptural truth.

How does this help us to break free of the mood-swing cycles? Keeping our heart includes making a decision to stop condemning ourselves for our failures. Instead, we will want to continually focus on the truth that there is no condemnation for those who are in Christ Jesus (Romans 8:1). Because of Christ's sacrifice on our behalf, we can rely upon God's promises for the power to change our responses. The apostle Paul tells us, "I am confident of this very thing, that He who began a good work in you will perfect it until the day of Christ Jesus" (Philippians 1:6).

GETTING OFF THE EMOTIONS-GO-ROUND

So how would keeping the heart work in Tasha's case? In the scenario described earlier, Tasha had half an hour to get Susan to the play, and Susan was nervous. Suddenly Tasha thought that adding a few sequins would add a nice touch to Susan's costume.

Once Tasha realizes that her perfectionism is driving her mood swings, she should recognize that her desire to sew on some extra sequins is an alarm of sorts. She should respond to this awareness with prayer, understanding that she doesn't have the power to change herself apart from God's grace. She should remind herself that her goal is to glorify God, not herself, and to help her daughter learn to do the same by controlling her emotions. Having realized this truth, Tasha needs to resist the impulse to add sequins to the costume and, instead, to concentrate on helping Susan cope with her nervousness on the way to the play.

Biblical counselor and author David Powlison says, "Only one thing is strong enough to overpower a stormy life: what God promises to do in and through Jesus Christ. . . . We escape ourselves by learning a lifestyle of intelligent repentance, genuine faith, and specific obedience."[5] Did you notice the "my part/His part" emphasis in Powlison's words?

THE BENEFIT OF STRUCTURE

In addition to the discipline of keeping the heart, women who are serious about gaining control over their mood swings should look carefully at their personal habits and schedules. What doctors call "structure" is the simple practice of keeping regular hours, eating regular meals, and disciplining yourself to not do things you know can cause you to become irritable, negative, or discouraged. For one woman this might mean not drinking coffee just before bedtime. For another, it might mean not eating salty food or sweets during her premenstrual time. And all of us could benefit from committing ourselves to a healthy diet, regular meals, exercise, and eight hours of sleep each night.

In C. S. Lewis's fiction novel *The Screwtape Letters*, a "senior tempter" gives this advice on temptation to a less-experienced devil:

> Never let him notice the medical aspect. Keep him wondering what pride or lack of faith has delivered him into your hands when a simple enquiry into what he has been eating or drinking for the last twenty-four hours would show him whence your ammunition comes.[6]

So often we fail to anticipate problems that could be prevented by careful attention to the kinds of physical issues that can tempt us toward a spiritual fall!

On the other hand, some women are very susceptible to the temptation to see their hormonal struggles (or symptoms of physical exhaustion or illness) as evidence of serious spiritual failure. While it is important to look at our heart when we struggle with moods, we also need to remember to consider the contribution that bodily weakness may make to our problems. If you tend to be especially hard on yourself when you are premenstrual, this advice is for you!

ABUSING YOUR BODY

When it comes to our moods, some of us are especially tempted to turn to overeating, taking extra medicines, or drinking too much alcohol. These choices will worsen the mood-swing cycle in the long run, regardless of how they may make us feel in the short run. We need to avoid these temptations to sin with our bodies the same way that we avoid temptations to sin with our emotions: by asking God to empower us against these habitual responses, by examining our hearts for sinful motives, and by choosing to respond differently.[7]

WHAT IF YOU HAVE SPECIAL CHALLENGES?

Biblical truth is universal. By this we mean that all of it applies to all of us, regardless of our particular circumstances. Some of us have physical challenges, whether they are a tendency toward manic psychosis, a tendency to have severe premenstrual symptoms, or a serious physical disease characterized by pain or disability. These challenges may make obedience to God's Word more difficult for us, but they do not exempt us from this responsibility. In fact, practicing the discipline of keeping the heart and choosing to live in a more structured way can improve your emotional stability even if you continue to take medicines to help stabilize your mood.

Our gracious heavenly Father created us and understands us completely (Psalms 103:14; 139:1–3). He knows our strengths and our weaknesses, and has promised us grace enough to meet all our challenges in a godly way. No matter what the problem, God will enable us to honor Him as we commit ourselves to understanding our hearts and obeying His commands.

GROWING IN YOUR FAITH

1. Do you struggle with mood swings before the onset of your period? What is your underlying heart attitude during this time? How might you better deal with the temptations that arise at this time? Some women find their emotions less overwhelming if they track their periods on a calendar. Knowing the date of the first day of your last period can help you watch for the instability that may arise during the last week before your next period is due. Other women find that

decreasing caffeine, chocolate, and salt before the onset of their period decreases their symptoms.

2. Are you finding menopause emotionally trying? Some women find that over-the-counter pain reliever PM formulas make them sleepy enough that their hot flashes don't wake them up. Better sleep at night leads to greater stability during the day. Other women choose estrogen replacement treatment, although you should be sure you do your homework and discuss this option carefully with your doctor, because serious side effects have been associated with such treatment.

3. Do you have mood swings most of the time? Is your pattern characterized by anger, fear, or some other emotion that alternates with depression? Do you tend to be irritable, or are you more likely to panic? Are you a perfectionist? What is your underlying heart attitude? How can understanding what motivates you help you battle your temptations?

4. What changes do you need to make in your schedule or personal habits so you are less tempted to give in to emotional storms?

5. Look at your use of medicines and alcohol with a suspicious eye. Do you need to make some changes here? If so, find a mature Christian woman who is willing to serve as an accountability partner, and ask her to hold you responsible for any changes you decide to make.

6. Summarize, in four or five sentences, what you learned in this chapter.

Margarita's Story

I have had Lyme disease since I was twelve. My doctor diagnosed me as having Schizoaffective Disorder (schizophrenia with mood swings), but I believe that an infection accompanying Lyme disease is what actually affected my brain.

I hear voices in my head that say awful things. At first medicine helped quiet the voices, but now my doctor can't find the right medicines to make them stay away completely. So I've had to do my best to honor and obey God even when the mean messages from these voices make me cranky and suspicious of other people. I used to bottle up everything inside me, but eventually I would burst out in anger. I have now learned to share with loved ones what is going on inside me so that I don't have to face it alone.

I try to trust the advice from my loved ones, because sometimes I have trouble discerning what is real and what is not. I've learned it is very important that I not trust myself because what seems to be true to me sometimes isn't. Trusting myself has gotten me into a lot of trouble in the past. Now, in the same way that a blind man trusts his sighted helper, I try to trust the people God has placed in my life.

I've also learned that I have to trust God first and foremost. I'm learning to test my thoughts against what the Bible says is true. I also walk close to God, reading my Bible every day and praying for strength to believe what is true and do the right things. And I've learned that even when I fail, Jesus always forgives me—no matter what.

Sometimes it is hard for me to endure with this problem. I would like to have a career and move away from home, or get married, as many of my friends from school have done. But I don't know when I will be able to do such things. I constantly remind myself that God is in control of my life, and that He has a purpose in my sufferings.

I pray that one day God will heal me. But if He does not, I still want to love and serve Him the best I can in the body He has given me. I'll keep on taking my medicines and do everything I can to be as healthy and stable as possible, and I'll trust Him to help me be the best person I can be in spite of my Lyme disease.

EIGHT

WHAT ABOUT COGNITIVE AND PERCEPTUAL PROBLEMS?

THOUGH OUR OUTER MAN IS DECAYING, YET OUR
INNER MAN IS BEING RENEWED DAY BY DAY.

2 Corinthians 4:16

PHINEAS GAGE WAS an energetic, efficient, and capable railroad construction foreman, a natural leader who was well liked by the men who worked under him. All this changed in 1848 after a freak accident caused by an explosion. A metal rod blasted through Phineas's left cheekbone and out the top of his skull with such force that it landed three hundred feet away! Amazingly, Phineas survived this severe brain injury, which wiped out much of the front left side of his brain. Even more astonishingly, he suffered no paralysis or loss of speech. But Phineas lost something even more valuable that day. "Gage," his coworkers and friends agreed, "was no longer Gage."

Phineas had always been a polite and considerate man, but after his recovery his friends found him terribly changed. He was now selfish, irritable, and prone to abusive outbursts of profanity. His doctor said it was as if he had lost the balance between "his intellectual faculty and animal propensities." He was erratic and unreliable and had difficulty thinking ahead and carrying out his plans. In short, he no longer demonstrated the abilities that made him an able foreman before his accident.

Eventually Phineas's unreliable and offensive behavior led to the loss of his job. He worked at menial jobs until his death from a seizure disorder eleven years later. Today his skull is on display at Harvard Medical School. Study of the nature of Phineas's injuries and his resulting disabilities has enabled doctors to understand the functions of the brain's frontal lobes, where Phineas's brain damage occurred.[1] Why did this damage change what seemed to be Phineas's core personality so radically?

BRAIN INJURIES AND DISEASES

One key theme we've repeated all through this book is that having a bad feeling, such as depression, isn't the same as having a disease. But we have also emphasized that there are diseases of the brain, just as there are diseases of the rest of our body. Brain diseases develop when the tissues of our brain are injured by illness or trauma. Some of the brain disorders that can produce problems similar in some ways to Phineas's include dementia (including Alzheimer's disease), traumatic brain injury (TBI), stroke, psychosis (including schizophrenia and mania), and autism. Most people with these diagnoses will not be as impaired as Phineas was, but some may be.

In this chapter we'll discuss the kinds of difficulties faced by women with these diseases or injuries, and consider how they can glorify God even if their brain doesn't work as it should. We hope this chapter will minister to women who have difficulty believing that they still have value in the eyes of God, their family, and their community because they are no longer able to do what they once did as a result of being afflicted by old age or some physical infirmity.

COGNITIVE-PERCEPTUAL PROBLEMS

Cognitive-perceptual (C-P) problem is our term for brain maladies that affect either a person's ability to think clearly (cognitive), ability to perceive reality clearly (perceptual), or both. But you don't need to develop a disease to experience mild C-P problems. Most of us suffer from memory loss as we get older. And normal aging may also be accompanied by what doctors call mild cognitive impairment (MCI), which is a more moderate kind of memory loss. Normal memory loss or MCI can affect how we feel about ourselves in very significant ways. It can be difficult to admit that you aren't as sharp as you used to be and that you need help. After we've looked at the various kinds of C-P problems that exist, we'll discuss the kinds of temptations that are faced by those who have these problems, and we'll present some concrete solutions.

DEMENTIA

Dementia is a severe senility, of which Alzheimer's disease is the best-known example, affecting thinking and perception, and it contains most of the elements that are found in varying degrees in the other C-P disorders. Although many women who are diagnosed with MCI will not go on to develop full-blown dementia, some will. When this happens, their MCI continues to worsen rather than level off.

By the time they are diagnosed, most women with dementia are already complaining of fairly severe problems with their memory, thought processes, and inability to learn new information. Please understand, however, that dementia is diagnosed when there is a severe case of memory loss. The fact that you can't remember where you placed your car keys (or that you can't find your car!) doesn't mean you're getting dementia.

A woman with dementia may also develop hallucinations (seeing or hearing things that are not really there). With these hallucinations can come wrong beliefs, called delusions, which she thinks are reality because of what she has seen or heard. She also will have impaired executive function, which is the ability to plan, set goals, anticipate problems, make use of information, initiate action, and manage time.

This makes it increasingly difficult for her to take part in the routine activities of daily life.

As the dementia progresses, she will struggle with behaviors that seem to straddle the borderland between sin and physical impairment. For instance, she may begin to have difficulty controlling her impulses. Distressingly, sometimes this will include impulses she has never surrendered to before, such as profanity or stealing. She may become more emotionally unstable and prone to anger, fits of inconsolable crying, overeating, and making impulsive purchases. Even if she was very wise before the onset of her disease, her ability to see her contribution to her own problems and make good decisions (what doctors term "insight and judgment") will decrease over time. She will have a short attention span, be easily overstimulated by things going on around her, and have decreased alcohol tolerance.

If she doesn't realize that she needs to stop drinking, she may have trouble with drunkenness. If she doesn't realize she is no longer a safe driver, she may have car accidents. A previously kind, gentle Christian woman may begin to get into fights with strangers. Those who have known her for decades will feel as if she has undergone a total personality change. They will say, "It's just not like her," or "It's like she's not even the same person."

What's Going on Here?

From a biblical perspective, how are we to understand such a transformation? Memory and executive function losses seem to make sense as consequences of a brain disease, but what are we to make of the development of behaviors that most people agree have their origin in the heart and not the physical brain? To better understand the process by which a sick body may affect a person's heart, we need to return again to our biblical theology of emotions.

You'll remember from chapter 1 that our behaviors develop as a result of what is going on in our hearts. In chapter 2 we saw that the body can affect the heart, and the heart can also affect the body. Because the body can affect the heart, it makes sense that a sick brain can affect the heart's activity in ways that a healthy brain wouldn't.

The heart, in turn, can affect a person's behavior. This can lead to disturbing changes in a person.

We've discussed the need to pay attention to what is in our hearts and to control our responses. But what happens if our capacity to keep our hearts is affected by a physical disease? This can happen with diseases of other organs besides the brain. For instance, a woman with pneumonia can become delirious with fever. As she receives antibiotics and her fever comes under control, she will regain conscious control of her mind, sometimes remembering the crazy things she saw and thought while she was ill. She may be mortified to recall that she hit her doctor while he was examining her. Generally, a woman who has recovered from a high fever will say that when she was sick she was unable to think clearly and understand what was happening to her, no matter how hard she tried.

In pneumonia, the infection and fever processes cause temporary changes in the brain, causing it to malfunction for a time. This ends when the infection is brought under control and normal brain function returns. But in dementia, the brain itself is sick. Just as in the case of delirium due to fever, in dementia, a sick brain presents incorrect information to the heart. The heart's thoughts, conclusions, and choices are influenced by the wrong information it receives.

Because there is no cure for dementia, the problem will not go away as it does when a fever disappears. Rather, it worsens. Over time, a woman who is misperceiving her environment because of dementia may develop delusions or wrong beliefs that make sense only to her.

Renowned biblical counselor Dr. Jay Adams says this about such errors in perception: "Error in judgment (leading to error in action) at times may result from physical impairment. . . . Error, in such cases, is neither the result of willful misreading or misleading, nor does it stem from sinful patterns of life."[2]

The Downward Pull of Indwelling Sin

The Bible teaches that because of Adam's disobedience toward God in the Garden of Eden, we are born with a sinful nature, and thus our hearts are naturally inclined toward doing wrong. When we are born again we are given new hearts; our natures are renewed and transformed by the power of the Holy Spirit. We are "new creatures" in Christ (2 Corinthians 5:17). Yet even then, sin continues to dwell in us for as long as we live (Romans 7:20), sometimes exerting a powerful influence on us (what Paul describes as "a law of sin" in verse 23). This gives rise to an ongoing struggle with sin in the life of every believer. We are instructed to keep or guard our hearts because we are still naturally inclined toward sin, even though our new birth in Christ has given us the ability to resist it.

In dementia patients, a problem with self-control may develop as the brain's deterioration progressively affects the heart's activity. If a woman's ability to keep her heart is compromised by this physical illness of the brain, indwelling sin may urge her toward behaviors she would never have carried out before. Of course, as fallible human beings, we are not capable of determining how much of a dementia patient's undesirable behavior originates from willful sin and how much is related in some way to the person's brain damage. Our gracious, righteous, and merciful God alone understands the heart, and He will be the final judge of each person's behavior. Christians, even those with dementia, can rest in the glorious truth that all their sin has already been judged in Christ. No Christian need fear that something they might say or do in their dementia will fall outside of the atonement purchased for them by Jesus Christ.

Does this mean a person with dementia is never guilty of sin? Of course not. People with brain diseases sin in the same ways as people with diseases in other parts of the body do. A woman who believes that the CIA wants to kill her is not sinning if she runs from someone she thinks is following her, but if she calls her husband a bad name because he tries to stop her, she has given way to sinful anger and profanity. However, most situations are not as clear-cut as this simple example. In real life the boundary between physical disability and sin can be very difficult to determine.[3] Great discernment and mercy is called for from all who help people suffering from dementia.

Dr. Adams reminds us that "one must deal with perceptual problems as well as any other physical impairments, righteously, not sinfully."[4] This means, among other things, that although a woman struggles with knowing what is real, or with controlling her impulses, she still needs to strive to the best of her ability to do what is right in the face of her misperception. We will discuss this in more detail later in this chapter.

OTHER C-P DISORDERS

Interestingly, all C-P problems that doctors attribute to a diseased brain have some features in common with dementia, even when the brain is sick for different reasons, in different areas, or even for as yet unknown reasons. We've already taken a detailed look at dementia. Let's look next at the specific cognitive problems seen in various disorders, and then look more closely at disorders that produce serious perceptual problems.

COGNITIVE PROBLEMS

Loss of executive function, memory, self-control, insight, and judgment are especially associated with physical disease or injury that involves the frontal lobes of the brain. The best example of this is the lack of inhibition that often results from a head injury, although these types of problems can also occur with frontal lobe stroke, dementia, schizophrenia, and autism. The classic historical example of frontal lobe TBI is the 1848 injury to Phineas Gage. We've already discussed how this changed him.[5]

Head injuries and dementia can also cause some loss of knowledge and abilities, as can strokes. These ailments can also cause paralysis and loss of speech, depending upon where the injury occurs in the brain. In schizophrenia, movement and speech are less affected, but loss of knowledge and abilities often occurs, and those who have had schizophrenia for a long time can develop movement disorders as well. Autism can impair speech when it is severe, and can be accompanied by cerebral palsy or more mild movement disorders. Many people with autism also have some degree of mental retardation, but some have a normal or even high IQ.

Patients with executive function and self-control problems are sometimes given the same medicines that are given to patients with psychotic disorders. These medicines help inhibit undesirable behavior and emotional instability, but they do not help improve executive function, insight, or judgment. Medicines are now available that help slow cognitive decline for those who have MCI and dementia. They can help slow memory loss and may help executive function if taken early enough in the course of a dementing illness.

PERCEPTUAL PROBLEMS

Psychotic disorders such as schizophrenia[6] and mania are accompanied by perceptual problems, and dementia can include perceptual problems too. Like these disorders, brain injuries caused by trauma or stroke may cause patients to experience hallucinations. By contrast, people with autism never have hallucinations.

Schizophrenia

Schizophrenia was the focal point of the motion picture *A Beautiful Mind*. In the movie we observe the deterioration of a brilliant mathematician, John Nash, who has schizophrenia. He thought he saw people chasing him, and he heard voices that told him that he had special powers and that only he could protect America from attack by enemies. Over time Nash suffered from delusions, including the belief that enemies were out to get him. His "crazy" behavior was understandable to viewers as they watched the story unfold because they were able to see what he was seeing and relate to what he was feeling.

Actor Russell Crowe won an Academy Award for his realistic portrayal of John Nash. In the movie he demonstrated the stiff posture and the abnormal movements that are characteristic of schizophrenia as the disease progresses. He also portrayed the cognitive toll that schizophrenia can cause as he struggled to do math in the grip of the confusion caused by the disease. In real life, Nash had won the Nobel Peace Prize for work he had done before he suffered from hallucinations and delusions. After years of brain disease he became a shadow of his former self intellectually, although he still knew more math than most of us do!

There are medicines that can help calm a patient's thoughts and suppress hallucinations, and they can help stabilize the progression of schizophrenia. Some doctors think that taking these medications faithfully may help prevent relapses and keep further damage from occurring to the brain. There is no known cure for schizophrenia.

It is possible for a person to have an isolated episode of psychosis (perhaps precipitated by sleep loss or drug abuse), recover, and never have another episode. But the majority of people with a first episode of psychosis will prove to have a permanent brain disorder and will continue to struggle with confused thoughts, emotions, and hallucinations. If you have been diagnosed with schizophrenia and have relapsed after a trial of slow, medically supervised medicine withdrawal, you will probably need to continue taking your medicines.

Psychotic Mania

Bipolar I is diagnosed when a person has a history of psychotic mania. People with psychotic mania can go for days, and sometimes weeks, without sleeping. They are excited, extremely talkative, and out of touch with reality in a very dramatic way. They usually have hallucinations and delusions, but they behave differently than people with schizophrenia, who tend to be quieter and to act less on their crazy thoughts. A person with mania might think she is the best friend of the president of the United States and attempt to make repeated collect calls to the White House, day and night, to speak to him. She might think that her house is bugged or stay awake for weeks watching for an assassin. Someone who is in an excited state like this often spends money impulsively and with poor judgment. This person could probably be persuaded to buy the Brooklyn Bridge! Her behavior may cause her to lose her job, or she may even be arrested for breaking the law while attempting to act on her crazy beliefs.

Depression is common after bouts of psychotic mania, and it seems that this may be related to financial, interpersonal, or legal problems that resulted from choices made while the person was not in her right mind. Embarrassment over remembered behavior, or even simple exhaustion from weeks of sleep deprivation, may also be factors. Because depression frequently follows psychotic mania, this condition originally came to be known as manic depression, now commonly known as bipolar disorder.

Mania can be precipitated by sleep deprivation, head injury, drug abuse, and the use of psychiatric medicines. It also sometimes occurs in people who have none of the risk factors that can bring on mania, and it can recur over and over in some people for reasons that are not completely understood. Medicines that help stabilize mania can be lifesaving for people who experience recurrent episodes. Because it is possible for a woman diagnosed with manic depression to have not really had an episode of psychotic mania, we believe that slow, supervised medicine withdrawal should be tried in those whose history is in question, and in those who have had only one episode.

SHOULD PATIENTS WITH C-P
DISORDERS TAKE MEDICINES?

Throughout this book, we have emphasized that emotions and behavior have their start in the heart, and that to improve them a person needs to change the way she thinks about herself and God. We have also mentioned that in many cases, medicines can cause more problems than they solve.

But we also want to make it very clear that if you suffer from a C-P disorder, we do not believe that your *personal* sin is responsible for all the disturbances you are experiencing. Remember that we are also all affected by Adam's sin in the Garden of Eden. This sin can affect our choices if we are making perceptual mistakes, even if we are working as hard as we can to keep our hearts right. If this is true for you, we suggest that you may need your medicines to help you think as clearly as possible.

Does this mean that you couldn't ever try going without medicines if you haven't tried already? Of course not. Our God is gracious and merciful. No one can understand all His ways. He might heal

you of your disease, or you may have suffered from a temporary disturbance, or you may have been incorrectly diagnosed. By all means
try to avoid the problems that can be associated with the use of medicines if you can. But medicines are part of God's gracious provision
for those with diseases, and they can help minimize their potentially
devastating impact. When we find we must take medicines for a disease in any part of our body, we should take them prayerfully and
with faith, always looking to God as the true source of our improvement. He is glorified when we do this.

We also want to remind you again that if you decide to stop
taking your medicines, you should do so only with your doctor's
agreement and under supervision. Withdrawal from the use of any
psychiatric medicine can cause mood instability, so it should be done
slowly and under the care of someone competent to recognize if all is
not going well. For more information on asking your doctor about
medicine withdrawal, please refer to appendix C. Please note that we
don't believe that women with dementia should ever stop taking any
medicines that improve their cognitive function unless their doctor
recommends it, because these drugs may help slow or stop the decline
of cognitive functions. (As of this writing, these medicines include
Aricept, Cognex, and Exelon.)

SPECIAL TEMPTATIONS PATIENTS
WITH C-P PROBLEMS FACE

While a person's sin is not responsible for all behavior that results
from perceptual errors, we must point out that there is the possibility
of willful sins that women with C-P problems may find especially
tempting. Keep in mind that patients with brain dysfunctions can
make a deliberate choice to sin, just as patients with diseases in other
bodily organs can. Let's consider some temptations that are "common
to man" (1 Corinthians 10:13) whether a person is experiencing some
loss of abilities with age or is suffering from a C-P problem.

DENIAL

When we have a problem, one of our most common human responses is to say, "Problem? There's no problem here!" Those who suffer from memory loss are often quick to deny their ailment. It's easy to see why this might happen. Recognizing that you're losing some of your abilities can be terribly threatening. You might not want to admit it, even to yourself.

What kinds of thoughts might such an admission trigger in you? That you are past your prime? That your years of making a contribution to your world have come to an end? That you have nothing more to look forward to but more loss—loss of independence, of dignity, and ultimately, of life?

Dear sister, don't succumb to such thoughts! The vast majority of women who experience memory loss will not progress to severe disease. Yet even if you do, you can have the assurance God will be with you and will glorify Himself even in your loss.

If you are affected by memory loss, don't let it affect your thoughts about your value to God. You may think you are of less value, but to think such thoughts is to follow your emotions instead of being guided by the truth, and this will only compound whatever physical problems you have. The truth is that your value never was based upon what you were able to do, even in your prime.

The Bible tells us that our worth is based upon our status as persons made in the image and likeness of God—and especially upon our adoption into God's family through our new birth in Christ. If God has ordained that we lose some of our ability to glorify Him in the ways we used to, this does not mean that our usefulness to others or our value to God diminishes. As we continue to respond to God in faith—to the limits of our ability, whatever that ability might be—He is pleased with us. Remember that God does not base His assessment of us upon our appearance or contributions. Rather, He looks on our heart (1 Samuel 16:7).

God wants us to respond to problems, even big problems, with prayerful and trustful faith in Him. When we deny that we have a problem and refuse help, we are only fooling ourselves. We are also depriving ourselves of the help and comfort that those who love us may long to provide.

LYING AND HIDING

It is sad when we resort to lying and covering up evidence of memory loss for fear of what others might think if they knew about our problem. Not only is lying an offense before a holy God, but it also places a barrier between our loved ones and us. When we lie to them, we are saying with our behavior that they are our enemies. We communicate the same thing when we refuse our loved ones' help and advice, or pretend that nothing is wrong with us.

ANGER

Another common response to memory loss is anger. We may be tempted to blame others for our difficulties and respond with anger, or we may take out our anger on those whom we love. When we respond this way, we will end up driving our loved ones further away from us.

CAN PATIENTS WITH SEVERE C-P DISORDERS GLORIFY GOD?

When we think of glorifying God, we tend to think of doing a great work for Him, don't we? Many of us want to bring honor and praise to Him through our wisdom, our work, our orderly homes, our obedient children, and our ministry.

Yet did you know we can also glorify God by patiently enduring through our suffering? Just because your life is disorderly on account of a cognitive or perceptual problem doesn't mean you can no longer glorify God.

Joni Eareckson Tada, who has learned much about patience through her four decades of quadriplegia, reminds us that even those who are no longer able to interact with the outside world because of their disabilities are still able to glorify God before the angels, who can see their faithful Christian walk. Ephesians 3:10 says that God's purpose is that His "manifold wisdom . . . might now be made known through the church [that's us] to the rulers and authorities [the angels] in the heavenly places."

Joni tells us of her friend John McAlister, who suffers paralysis from a degenerative neurological disease and lives alone in a nursing home:

> God's purpose is to teach millions of unseen beings about Himself; and we are—John McAlister is—a blackboard upon which God is drawing lessons about Himself for the benefit of angels and demons. God gets glory every time the spirit world learns how powerful His everlasting arms are in upholding the weak. My friend's life is not a waste. Although not many people seem to care, someone—a great many someones—care more than John can imagine. . . . Each day we go on living means something. God is up to something good when it comes to our trials.[7]

Dear sister, others may not see the battle you wage inside of yourself. They may not understand how hard you are trying to improve in your areas of weakness. But God is glorified every time you seek to obey Him and place His glory ahead of your own. You may continue to struggle with memory problems, confusion, self-control, or delusions and hallucinations that seem so real to you. You may not be doing anything with your life that says you are important in the eyes of the world. But God's Word says you are of great value to the Lord, and that you are making a contribution, even if you can't see it yet.

The Blessed Hope

The Bible tells us that a day is coming when God will set right all the wrongs in our fallen world. On that day, Jesus Christ will return to earth to judge everyone who has ever lived. At His return, all the dead in Christ who have gone to heaven will rise to live forever in perfect, sinless, glorified bodies.

Have you been told that you are going to leave this earth no longer able to remember your dear husband or other loved ones? If you and your loved ones know Jesus Christ, one day you will rise from your graves to live forever with the Lord. You will never be confused again. Have you endured hallucinations? You will never see or hear them again. In the new heavens and earth, the paralyzed will walk. The blind will see. Those with autism will speak. Phineas Gage, if he knew Jesus Christ before his death, will rise not as the amiable man he was before his injury, but as a perfect man, formed in likeness to the one Perfect Man.

If we define our worth and the meaning of our lives on the basis of what we can and cannot do, then we are missing the big picture. The Bible tells us that our worth is found in Christ alone and our ultimate hope is the promise of eternity with Christ. On our first day in heaven, we will, for the first time ever, understand the true meaning and value of our lives. Dear challenged sister, wait in faith for that day!

GROWING IN YOUR FAITH

1. Do you have memory loss? Have you been tempted to lie about or minimize your disability? How can you apply the encouragements in this chapter to your situation?

2. Have you been told that you are developing dementia? How can you trust Christ for the grace to guard your heart? Can you find an accountability partner to help you with this? Are you tempted to be angry with or resent your loved ones or caregivers? How can you use the concepts in this chapter to change your heart attitude toward your losses?

3. Do you have psychosis? Can you find someone you trust to help you decide what is real and what is not? Can this person also function as an accountability partner to help you keep your heart?

4. If you have been diagnosed with Bipolar I or schizophrenia, have you ever tried medicine withdrawal? If not, consider discussing this with your doctor. If you have tried medicine withdrawal unsuccessfully, please trust in God's good purposes for you and continue taking your medicines.

5. Summarize, in four or five sentences, what you learned in this chapter.

NINE

ALL FOR THE GLORY OF GOD

NOT TO US, O LORD, NOT TO US, BUT TO YOUR
NAME GIVE GLORY BECAUSE OF YOUR LOVINGKIND-
NESS, BECAUSE OF YOUR TRUTH.

Psalm 115:1

IN JOHN CHAPTER 9, we come across one of the most hope-filled stories in all the Bible.

Begging every day in the dusty streets of Jerusalem, there was a man who had been born blind. He had never seen the sun, never enjoyed the glorious colors and beauty of the temple, never seen his mother's smile. From childhood, his existence was one of hopelessness, shame, and deprivation.

Not only had he been born with one of the most difficult disabilities a person can know; he had also suffered from being the object of scorn and ridicule. In those days, people with disabilities weren't helped and provided for. People who weren't physically whole were often taught their handicap was the direct result of their own sin or the sin of their parents. Can you imagine the suffering this man and his family experienced every day as the self-righteous religious leaders walked by him, holding up their robes so that they wouldn't be contaminated? The level of his despair and hopelessness undoubtedly grew day by day until he finally reconciled himself with reality: He was a hopeless sinner, he was hopelessly blind, and he was hopelessly excluded from the company of the blessed. Nothing was ever going to change for him.

But one day, radiance suddenly flared into this seemingly senseless and sunless life. As the man sat begging, he overheard an unusual conversation. A rabbi was walking by. "Who sinned," someone asked, "this man or his parents?" Although the blind man had probably heard this theological discussion before, he listened with interest as an answer was given that would turn his world upside down.

The rabbi, whose name was Jesus, answered, "It was neither that this man sinned, nor his parents; but it was so that the works of God might be displayed in him" (John 9:3). Jesus discarded the false teaching that suffering and sin were analogous and replaced it with His mercy, compassion, and delight in His Father's glory. Why did this man suffer all those years? It wasn't for his sin or the sins of his parents.[1] His blindness was for the glory of God, that His great lovingkindness might be known in him and also to us. What was the fundamental cause of his blindness? Simply put, it was the glory of God.

Right now you might be wondering how blindness could eventuate in God's glory. That's an appropriate question. Blindness glorifies God because it teaches us about our own natural inabilities and of the power and ability that belongs to God alone. It tells us that without the direct intervention of the Spirit of God, each of us is just like this blind beggar: hopelessly excluded from holiness, cursed and under the wrath of God. But the awesome truth that we can all embrace now is that the Light has come, and He's given us what we could never give ourselves because we were spiritually blind. Jesus made this plain later in John 9 when He told the Pharisees that they were the truly blind ones (verses 39–41). To those who become Christians, God has given spiritual eyes so that we can know and understand His truth. We too were once blind, like the beggar in John 9, but now we see!

THE GLORY OF GOD AND YOU

Because you've persevered through this book, we know you're serious about your faith and you're serious about wanting to discover God's help. We're thankful this is the case. We also imagine that the motivating questions of your life are, "What does God want from me in this?" or, "How can I best bring praise and honor to His name through this?" These desires on your part are delightful assurances of God's work in you. In this, our final chapter together, we'd like to share some thoughts about God's method of change in a person's life and then encourage you in your calling to glorify Him.

In this book, we've built a foundational way for you to think about the troubling emotions that plague you. Rather than seeing these distressing emotions simply as the result of imbalanced brain chemistry, deficient genes, or misfiring brain synapses, we've encouraged you to view them from a different and consistently biblical perspective. In regard to your essential nature, you've learned that you are a person with both an outer, visible body and an inner, invisible mind or heart. You've also come to see that God's good will for us frequently includes suffering, as it did for His Son. And we've mentioned initial steps you can take as you seek to change the way you think and respond to the trouble in your life.

We know that these propositions (and our methods for achieving true heart change) fly in the face of the modern philosophy of biological materialism and even the fleeting promises of trouble-free living our society suggests. We know that emotional pain (in whatever form it might take) is viewed as an enemy to flee from rather than a tutor to learn from or a companion to be enriched by. In calling your emotional suffering a tutor or a companion, we aren't saying that suffering should simply be embraced without a fight. Contentment in difficulties doesn't mean mere blind acceptance; it means that we're to battle humbly and obediently against our problems, always echoing our Lord's prayer of submission: "Nevertheless, not my will, but yours, be done" (Luke 22:42 ESV). So in the rest of this chapter, let's take a closer look at God's method of changing us and then discover how we can persevere in this race we've been called to run as we lean on the strength of the Lord.

Participating in God's Work

It's interesting to note the method Jesus used to heal the blind beggar. He made mud out of dirt He had mixed with His saliva and put it on the man's eyes. Then Jesus told him, "Go, wash in the pool of Siloam" (verse 7). The Lord asked the man to walk through Jerusalem all the way to the Pool of Siloam and then wash the mud from his eyes.

Why would Jesus ask a blind person to walk all the way to a pool for his sight to be restored? Why didn't He just heal the beggar where he sat? We don't know the exact reasons for the Lord's action, but we do know this: The Lord's penultimate purpose in this man's life was His own glory, and asking the man to participate (and do something that seemed both foolish and difficult) brought the glory to the Lord.

Will You Go and Wash?

What would your response have been to Christ's command to go and wash? Perhaps you would have been desperate enough to do whatever He said in the hopes of being able to see again. Without a doubt, even though the command to walk to the pool probably seemed absurd to the blind man, he knew that he couldn't be choosy when it came to an opportunity to be healed. And so he went . . . and he was able to see for the first time.

As we consider the blind man's healing, we want to think very carefully about his participation in it. It was the *power of the Lord*, not the man's personal faith or obedience, that caused him to acquire his sight. But God did use the man's faith and obedience as the means to accomplish his healing.

Here's an example of what we're talking about when we say that God uses *means*. We all agree that God can, at any time, choose to save people and make them His own. He can do this because He is sovereign and the hearts of all people, even a king, are in His hands (Proverbs 21:1). But God usually doesn't save people "out of the blue," without sending someone as an evangelist or witness to be His messenger. God uses believers who serve as His representatives when He reaches out to the lost. As the prophet Jonah proclaimed, "Salvation is from the Lord!" (Jonah 2:9). But God uses a messenger when He leads someone to salvation (Romans 10:14).

God can (and might!) choose to miraculously deliver you from your painful thoughts and emotions. Or He might use your faithful (though imperfect and faltering) obedience as the instrument or means through which He brings change to your life. Although we do believe that God can instantaneously deliver you from your fear or depression as an independent act of His grace, that's not the way He usually works, and it's not the way change usually occurs, according to the New Testament.

Sanctification, the slow change into Christlikeness that God accomplishes in us through the work of the Spirit, is a *process.* Typically, this change is realized as we take halting steps in faith while He works His change in us. It's through this process that we learn to walk by faith, see triumph in defeat, and rest wholly on the perfect obedience of Another. It's also in this process that we become more like Him and the fruit that flows from our life is filled with sweetness.

WHAT THE BIBLE SAYS ABOUT CHANGE

Unlike the "five easy steps" and "magic cures" that the media bombards us with every day, the Bible teaches us that sanctification is a lifelong process that involves setting aside the old self and putting on the new:

> That, in reference to your former manner of life, you lay aside the old self, which is being corrupted in accordance with the lusts of deceit, and that you be renewed in the spirit of your mind, and put on the new self, which in the likeness of God has been created in righteousness and holiness of the truth. (Ephesians 4:22–24)

In the verses that follow, Paul tells his readers how to conquer certain sinful practices and troubling emotions such as lying, anger, stealing, unkind speech, wrath, and unforgiveness. He counseled them that true change takes place on three levels: 1) the outward putting off or ceasing of old thoughts and behaviors; 2) the internal transformation of the mind; and 3) the deliberate putting on or assuming of new, godly thoughts and behavior.

GOD'S WAY OF CHANGING US

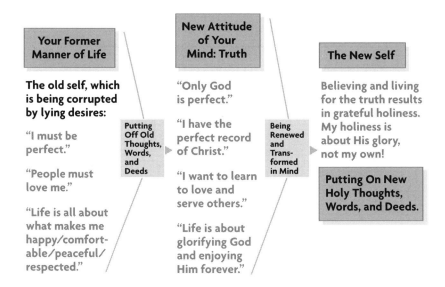

For instance, in Ephesians 4:25, Paul tells the liar that he must not only stop lying (putting off this false behavior), but he must also start telling the truth (putting on new, godly behavior), and that he must view those whom he might be tempted to lie to as his neighbors or part of the body of Christ. Instead of thinking of these three steps as happening consecutively, think about them as all happening concurrently: Stop lying, tell the truth, and see others as family members—all at the same time.

Paul then tells the person who steals to stop stealing (putting off) and to start working and giving (putting on), all the while thinking about others who are in need more than himself (being renewed in his mind). God's power transforms the thief into a diligent worker and generous giver who comes to see himself as a person God might use to bless others.

In verses 31–32 Paul speaks to those who are given to anger and unkind actions and words: "Let all bitterness and wrath and anger and clamor and slander be put away from you, along with all malice. Be kind to one another, tender-hearted, forgiving each other, just as God in Christ also has forgiven you." At the same time that an angry person was to change his thinking, he was to think deeply about how Christ had forgiven him and then let that reality motivate all his change.

Like the liar, the thief, the angry, unforgiving person, and the blind beggar, the Lord can and will transform us as we respond in faith to His Word. Just like them, we can seek (by His grace) to respond in faith to the truths He's brought to us, and we can expect that He will faithfully encourage, change, and free us. Even if you've been deeply sinned against by others (as the blind beggar had been), God says that His transforming grace is sufficient. In all our working for God and with Him, although He does call us to do our part, it's His strength (and not ours) that will win the day and bring us full freedom (Philippians 2:12–13).

The question we want to pose to you now is simply this: Are you willing to go and wash? Are you willing to traverse the streets of faith, sometimes feeling lost and hopeless, sometimes tripping over steps you forgot were there, putting one foot in front of the other, feeling foolish and embarrassed, and continue on even when you're beginning to wonder if you're making any headway at all? If you are, then God is already working in you to give you the faith and strength you'll need for this journey.

THE JOURNEY TOWARD CHANGE

Whenever we get ready to go on a journey, we take time to think about what we might need while we're traveling. In the same way, you'll want to make sure you're remembering everything you'll need as you travel from entanglement in your troubling emotions to godliness, fruitfulness, and rest in His transforming power.

Second Peter 1:2–8 provides us with a checklist of sorts for this journey:

> Grace and peace be multiplied to you in the knowledge of God and of Jesus our Lord; seeing that His divine power has granted to us every-thing pertaining to life and godliness, through the true knowledge of Him who called us by His own glory and excellence. For by these He has granted to us His precious and magnificent promises, so that by them you may become partakers of the divine nature, having escaped the corruption that is in the world by lust.
>
> Now for this very reason also, applying all diligence, in your faith supply moral excellence, and in your moral excellence, knowledge, and in your knowledge, self-control, and in your self-control, perse-verance, and in your perseverance, godliness, and in your godliness, brotherly kindness, and in your brotherly kindness, love. For if these qualities are yours and are increasing, they render you neither useless nor unfruitful in the true knowledge of our Lord Jesus Christ.

The goal that the Lord has set out for us is wonderfully daunting: By becoming partakers of His nature, we can now live a godly and meaningful life overflowing with fruitfulness! This, and nothing less, is the goal of God's work in our life. He wants to share His character and nature with us, and although we're called to participate in this transformation, all our efforts would be futile without the astonish-ing power of the Spirit to change us. Like the leopard, we can't change our spots (Jeremiah 13:23). But it's also true that He's called us to respond in faithful obedience, even when the change seems impos-sible. Can you give yourself a new nature? No, but He can, and He calls you to participate in this change. And as you respond in faithful obedience, you'll find yourself becoming someone new.

It Begins with Knowledge

Let's consider our part in this transformation by looking more closely at Peter's counsel to us. He tells us, first of all, that we need knowledge. The kind of knowledge we need is a personal knowledge about God—it's a knowledge that reveals His holiness to us, and the purposes of the life, death, burial, and resurrection of His Son. This is the most important information anyone could ever acquire.

- Can you articulate the gospel story? (If not, please turn to appendix A right away.)
- Do you know why Jesus died?
- How does that truth affect you in your difficulties today? Does the reality that He died to give you new life speak to your heart?
- Do you know you've been changed by His transforming power?

It Includes Everything We Need

As Peter continues, he tells us that if we're in Christ, we've been given everything we need for life and godliness. What that means is that although we aren't perfect (or sinless), if the Holy Spirit is residing in us (and He does indwell every true believer), then we have everything we need to live godly lives. We don't have to search endlessly for the magic cure for our problems. *Everything we need to grow in a life of godliness has been given to us.* These gifts were purchased for us by our Savior's perfect obedience and suffering in our place. If godliness and the divine life are our goals, then God has given us the means we need to make it to our journey's destination.

- Have you been looking for a magic formula or secret key to help you overcome your painful emotions? Where have you looked?
- What has your goal been as you've sought to change? Has it been godliness, or just freedom from pain?
- Do you believe Peter was right when he said that everything we need is found in God's promises to us?

It's Supported by God's Word

Peter goes on to tell us where this powerful knowledge and ability to change comes from: "His precious and magnificent promises" (verse 4). God's Word is so powerful that it can burn away all our self-delusions and hammer our resistant hearts and make them soft and pliable (Jeremiah 23:29). It can enable us to understand the deepest thoughts and intentions of our own heart (Hebrews 4:12), and it can cause us to grow in godliness (1 Peter 2:2). In fact, everything we need to know about how to love God and our neighbor is included there (Matthew 22:36–40). Because God is faithful to perform all His promises, we can be assured that He's going to complete His work in us (Philippians 1:6).

- Do you believe the Bible answers every question you have about life and godliness?
- Do you know what God has promised to do for you as His child? Which one of those promises is most meaningful to you?
- Do you go to the Scriptures expecting to receive not only information but also the power that you need to live for Him every day?
- Do you see that one of the reasons Scripture was given to us is so we can escape the lies and resulting death that our strong desires create?

It Involves Putting on Character Qualities

Finally, Peter provides for us a checklist of character qualities to put on. As we think again about Paul's teaching in Ephesians, we can see how Peter is talking about the same method of change: We're to put off every sinful desire (and the actions that flow from them). We're to put off every lie that we've believed and every faithless pursuit, and in their place, we're to put on:

- Moral excellence: Thoughts, words, and deeds that reflect the virtues and perfections of Jesus Christ. We're to obey and trust that God will enable us to live in such a glorious way.
- Knowledge: The journey we're on is one of continual learning. Every day our goal should be to get to know Him better, to

understand more of His holiness and love, and to learn more of His ways. Have you pursued a continual growth in your understanding (2 Peter 3:18)?

- Self-control: The Holy Spirit produces this character quality as a result of His work in our lives (Galatians 5:23). Although the word *self* in self-control seems to denote this is done in our own power, the truth is that our will must be moved on by "the operation of the Spirit of God."[2]

- Perseverance: It's wonderful that perseverance, or the ability to cheerfully and patiently endure difficulty, comes right after self-control. Whenever we fail in our efforts at self-control, we can rest in the knowledge that the Lord is patiently persevering in His work in our hearts. When we feel as if we're never going to get it right or be completely freed from our trials, that's the time when we need to remember His patience with us and rest in His loving arms. If we're His, we will persevere, and in this we can be confident.

- Godliness: This is "characterized by a Godward attitude" and "does that which is well pleasing to Him."[3] When you're struggling to put off your old destructive ways of thinking and wondering why all this is such a fight, remember that the goal of a fruitful life can be found by asking yourself this simple question: *What would please the Lord right now?* For instance, if you're tempted to give in to your compulsions or slide down into a pit of despair, ask yourself, "If pleasing the Lord is my goal today, what would that look like in this situation?"

- Brotherly kindness: One way you can please the Lord is by pursuing brotherly kindness or fond affection for others. If you find yourself struggling with an "angry mood," you can choose, by the strength and grace of the Spirit, to put that angry mood off and act with fond affection toward those around you.

- Love: We're to pursue love as a motivation for everything we do. As Paul said, the lack of love in our actions doesn't merely diminish their value; the lack of love renders our actions completely worthless (1 Corinthians 13:1–3). This is a frightening reality, isn't it? What's more, the kind of love we need doesn't come from us. Rather, the Spirit who indwells us can pour this love out into our hearts (Romans 5:5).

Here, in chart form, are the character qualities we're to put on:

Moral excellence	Before speaking or acting, what thoughts, words, or deeds might you "put on" that would reflect the beauties of Jesus Christ?
Knowledge	Are there truths you've learned that you'll need to embrace in place of the falsehoods that used to guide your emotions and behavior?
Self-control	Instead of giving in to what your emotions are telling you to do, what different, faith-filled actions could you take?
Perseverance	Sometimes obedience is nothing more than deciding to cheerfully and patiently plod along. Although we fail frequently, patience means we continue pursuing obedience, whether we can approve of ourselves or not.
Godliness	If you stop and ask yourself, "What would most please my Lord right now?" you'll find that He'll give you the wisdom and grace you need to follow through. Remember that godliness is not just "What would Jesus do?" but "What did He already do for you?"
Brotherly kindness	If you're not sure how the Lord wants you to respond in a particular situation, ask yourself, "What would being kind look like right now?"
Love	Love is the only power that's strong enough to overcome fear, anger, and hopelessness. This love doesn't originate in you, but comes to you from the Lord, who Himself is love. When wondering what to do, ask yourself, "What is the most loving thing I can do right now?"

What is God's promise to us as we cooperate with His plan and seek to put on these qualities of heart? He promises, "If these qualities are yours and are increasing, they render you neither useless nor unfruitful in the true knowledge of our Lord Jesus Christ" (2 Peter 1:8). We'll be useful and fruitful in response to this wonderful knowledge of our Lord.

OUR HOPE FOR YOU

Because you have persevered to the end of this book, we believe it's safe to say you want to be useful and fruitful for the Lord. You don't want everything He's taught you to come to nothing. You're longing to hear Him say, "Well done, good and faithful servant." If you desire to live a life that is faithful and overflowing with wonderful fruit, and you're willing to seek the Lord's help and obey Him in the pursuit, then yes, you will hear Him say that.

The struggle to put off old ways of thinking and put on new is difficult, but not impossible. If you didn't have the power of the Spirit, the Word of God, the atoning blood of your Savior, His daily prayers and intercession for you, and the providential rule of God in your life, then the change you're aiming for would be impossible. But you have all those benefits now, and so many more (see Psalm 103:1–18).

We don't know God's plans for your life, but we do know that if you call upon Him, He will help you (Psalm 145:18). Maybe the help will come in the form of perseverance as you struggle against your thoughts and feelings; maybe it will come in the form of a friend who will walk with you through this trial. The one truth we know for sure is that if we ask God for help, He's never late or too preoccupied to come to your aid.

And finally, although we don't know your specific challenge right now or how the Lord plans to deliver you, we do know this: He's working in this situation for His glory and your good. He's relentlessly pursuing you, as a loving husband would, to obtain from your life the glory, praise, and thanksgiving He deserves. He's pursuing that praise because He longs for your completeness and joy, and He knows that when your heart is wholly His, filled with songs of deliverance, you'll be filled with the joy and freedom you long for and that He alone provides.

I LOVE YOU, O LORD, MY STRENGTH

As our time together draws to a close, let us direct you to one final passage of Scripture. Can you say with David, "I love You, O Lord, my strength" (Psalm 18:1)? David spoke those words when he finally found deliverance from his enemy, King Saul. As you face wars with your enemies, whether they're the habitual thoughts that have taken up residence in your mind or distressing circumstances that never seem to change, can you say, "I love You, O Lord. Even now I see that You are my strength"?

David then goes on to describe the kind of strength he found in God. He said, "The Lord is my rock and my fortress and my deliverer, my God, my rock, in whom I take refuge; my shield and the horn of my salvation, my stronghold" (Psalm 18:2). Look at the words denoting strength in this verse: rock, fortress, deliverer, rock (again!), shield, the horn of my salvation, stronghold. He's making a point. The Lord inspired David to write these words after putting him through a difficult trial because He wanted you to read them. When you're tempted to give up and throw in the towel, believing that you'll never find victory, recite them: "You're my rock. Maybe I'm not strong and solid, but You are!" When you feel as if your emotions are being assailed from every direction, remind yourself: *I'm hiding in the fortress God has set up for me. I don't have to stand out here and take shots from my enemies. I can hide in Him!*

And remember this wonderful promise: "I call upon the Lord, who is worthy to be praised, and I am saved from my enemies" (Psalm 18:3). David described his struggle in this way: "The cords of death encompassed me, and the torrents of ungodliness terrified me. The cords of Sheol surrounded me; the snares of death confronted me" (verses 4–5). Then he proclaimed God's faithfulness to hear us: "In my distress I called upon the Lord, and cried to my God for help; He heard my voice out of His temple, and my cry for help before Him came into His ears" (verse 6). We know that God will hear your cry for help, and that He will bring you deliverance.

WHILE YOU WAIT FOR HEAVEN

Although Jesus performed a great deliverance for the blind beggar, this didn't solve all the beggar's problems. He had to endure the censure of the religious leaders and the desertion of his parents. God's deliverance of you may be similar. He may completely change your heart and life, but the truth is that you'll still have difficulties to face and trials to endure. We're saying this now just to remind you of something you already know so well: Life here on earth isn't heaven.

When we face constant difficulties with troubling emotions, we're tempted to think that if we could just feel better, everything would be okay. At the times when we start to do better and suddenly encounter trouble, we wonder, *What did I do wrong?* Please don't fall into this trap! For instance, if you've worked hard at putting off your anger or fear and then find yourself facing new difficulties in other areas, don't become discouraged. Although God is powerfully working to sanctify us, we won't be free from the problems of life anytime before heaven. In fact, the process of learning, growing, changing, failing, and then learning again is the very plan He's designed for us. Trials and difficulties are part of our life here, and God can use them to help us grow strong. And there is coming a day when all our problems will be gone. On that day, you'll find your heart singing with abandonment and inexpressible joy: "I love You, O Lord, my strength!" and you'll know that it was His strength, His grace, and His holy blood that brought you safely to your heavenly home. Take time now to pray, sing, reflect, and rejoice in what He is doing in your life. Remember, He is your strength!

GROWING IN YOUR FAITH

1. Please let us encourage you to stop now and say, "I love You, O Lord; You are my strength!" Add your own words and thoughts of God's goodness, love, and mercy, and spend time recounting how He has already been your deliverer and how He will yet deliver you.

2. Look back over the list of character qualities you'll need to "put on" in your journey (see page 194). Which ones do you have the most trouble with? Take time right now to pray about your need for God's strength in those areas.

3. Paul told Timothy that the goal of the instruction he brought was "love from a pure heart, a good conscience, and a sincere faith." In this book, that has been our goal too. Can you see any areas in which Paul's goal is different from yours? Perhaps your goal is just to feel better (not a wrong goal in itself), but Paul's goal is superior. Make it your goal to pray, "God, teach me how to love You and others with a pure heart. Grant me a love that springs from knowing that I don't have anything to hide from You or others; give me a sincere faith that's willing to admit when it's weak. Help me to always rest in the strength of the faithful obedience of Your Son. Thank You, Lord. I love You, my strength."

4. Summarize, in four or five sentences, what you learned in this chapter.

5. Look back over your answers to the summary question at the end of every "Growing in Your Faith" section in this book, and then write the four or five answers that were most meaningful to you. Pray that the Lord will help you remember them and help you work them out in your life.

APPENDICES

HOW YOU CAN KNOW IF YOU'RE A CHRISTIAN

IF YOU AREN'T a Christian, it will be impossible for you to understand and follow the truths that are contained in this book and experience the joy of God-empowered change. But that's not the most important reason for becoming a Christian.

Rather, the key reason is so that you can know the joy of peace with God and have the assurance that your sins are forgiven.

Many people attend church or try to live good lives, and assume that if they're basically nice and loving, God will accept them into heaven. But that's not the standard God gives us in the Bible.

First, it's important for us to understand that God is perfectly holy. That means He never thinks or does anything that is inconsistent with His perfection. He is pure and without fault of any kind. That's not because He gets up every morning and says, "I'll try to be good today."

In addition to being perfectly holy, God is just. He always sees that justice is served—which means that those who deserve punishment will always receive it in the end. If God allowed people to get away with breaking His laws, then He wouldn't really be holy.

In one sense, God's holiness and justice reassure us. The wicked people of this world, even though they seemingly have escaped judgment here on earth, will stand before their Creator and will receive exactly what they deserve. But, in another sense, God's holiness and justice should make us all uncomfortable. That's because, even though we may not be as bad as we could be, we know that we sin, and God hates sin.

Very simply speaking, *sin is any violation of God's perfect standards.* His standards are contained in the Bible and were summed up in the Ten Commandments in the Old Testament. Think for a moment about those commandments: Have you had any other gods in your life—that is, have you ever made anything a higher priority than God? Have you reverenced the Lord's Day and set it apart for Him? Have you always honored those in authority over you? Have you ever turned your back on someone who needed your protection? Have you ever desired someone who was not your spouse? Have you ever taken anything that wasn't yours? Have you ever told a lie or looked at something that someone else had and wanted it for yourself?

The Bible tells us that all have sinned (Romans 3:23). And there will come a time when you, too, will stand before God's judgment seat. But don't despair. If you admit you are a sinner, then there is hope for you, because God is not only holy and just; He's also merciful.

Though we are sinners, God still has immense love for us, and because of this, He made a way for you and me to come to Him. He did this without compromising His holiness and justice. You see, someone had to take the punishment for your sin. Someone had to die in your place. But who could do this and still maintain God's justice?

Every person who has ever lived has sinned and therefore has been disqualified from taking someone else's punishment because they deserved punishment of their own. Only one Man could take this punishment. Only one Man was perfectly sinless and completely undeserving of punishment. That Man was Jesus Christ. Jesus Christ was both God (making Him perfectly sinless) and Man (making Him suitable as our "stand-in"). The Bible teaches that because of God's love for humanity, He sent His Son, Jesus Christ, to die in our place. On the cross, Jesus took the punishment we deserved. Thus God's justice is served, and His holiness is upheld. That's why the Bible teaches that "while we were yet sinners, Christ died for us" (Romans 5:8).

Perhaps as you are reading this you know you are a sinner. What must you do? You must believe these truths about your sin and Christ's death for you on the cross, and you must ask God to forgive you of all your sins. You can do this through prayer. There aren't any special words that you must say. In fact, the Bible says "whoever will call on the name of the Lord will be saved" (Romans 10:13). You can pray to Him, asking Him to forgive your sin because of Jesus' sacrifice. You can ask Him to make you His own. The Bible says, "If we confess our sins, He is faithful and righteous to forgive us our sins and to cleanse us from all unrighteousness" (1 John 1:9).

Being a Christian has sometimes been called a "trust transfer." That you're a follower of Christ doesn't mean that you're good or that you have to vote a certain way. Rather, it means that you've completely stopped trusting in your own goodness to make yourself acceptable before the Lord. You're trusting in the goodness, ability, and wisdom of Another: Jesus Christ. He's been perfect in your place and has taken the punishment you deserved. He's paid it all; He's done it all. All you have to do is trust Him.

Now, if you have become a Christian, you will want to live for the Lord in a way that pleases Him. In order to know how to do that, you must begin reading His Word. A good place to begin is the gospel of John in the New Testament. As you read, pray that God will help you to understand His Word.

You will also want to find a good Bible-believing church and start attending it. A Bible-believing church is one that believes in the Trinity (that the Father, the Son, and the Holy Spirit are equally one God), believes that salvation is entirely a free gift of God, practices prayer and holiness, and believes that the Bible is the inspired Word of God (and no other books are on equal footing).

If you've become a Christian through the ministry of this book, we would love to know so that we can rejoice with you. Please write to us through the publisher: Moody Publishers, 820 N. LaSalle Boulevard, Chicago, IL 60610, or email authors@moody.edu. May God's richest blessings be yours as you bow humbly before His throne!

UNDERSTANDING MEDICINE DEPENDENCE, WITHDRAWAL, AND SIDE EFFECTS

DURING THE TWO WEEKS following her husband's death, Tracey felt sad and worried during the day and was unable to sleep at night. She went to her doctor, and he prescribed an antidepressant. After several months on the antidepressant, Tracey's doctor told her she could stop taking it because she felt so much better. But when she stopped, she became anxious and depressed again. Her doctor put her back on the antidepressant and referred her to a psychiatrist.

The psychiatrist increased the medicine dosage when Tracey failed to respond any more to the original dosage, and told Tracey that the return of her symptoms meant she was suffering from the disease of depression. Tracey did well on the increased dosage for about six months, but then she began struggling with depression again.

The doctor increased the dosage again, and a few days later Tracey became agitated and irritable, and had trouble sleeping. She became unusually talkative, made impulse purchases, and began getting into arguments at work. Her psychiatrist told her that her treatment for depression had unmasked her underlying disease of bipolar disorder, and started her on a mood-stabilizing medicine.

After a few months on both the antidepressant and mood stabilizer,

Tracey became depressed yet again, and her psychiatrist added a second antidepressant to the regimen. Tracey's depression did not improve when this third medicine was added, and she began hearing voices that told her she was ugly and everyone hated her. Her psychiatrist then added an antipsychotic medicine. Today Tracey no longer works, and receives disability compensation for her severe case of bipolar disorder.

We wish we could tell you that we are exaggerating the details of Tracey's story, but we have counseled a number of women who have experienced a sequence of events much like Tracey's. Some have gotten to the point where they can no longer live normal lives because of the tail-chasing that developed as their doctors responded to each new symptom by adding more medicines. This, of course, further masked and aggravated the problems that originated in their hearts rather than resolving them.

In the pages that follow, we'll discuss dependence, withdrawal, and the very serious problem of medication-induced violence and suicide. Then we'll describe common side effects that can occur in each general class of psychiatric medicines. We hope this information will help you to make a more informed decision about whether these medicines are right for you.

DEPENDENCE AND WITHDRAWAL

Dependence (also known as *addiction*) is a physical state that occurs when your body has become accustomed to receiving a medicine that has habit-forming potential. *Withdrawal* is the unpleasant physical reaction that occurs when you abruptly stop taking a medicine after your body has become accustomed to receiving it. If you become dependent upon a habit-forming medicine, increasing dosages will be required over time to continue to produce the same effect. Most of us are aware that you can become dependent upon street drugs and pain medicines, but many don't realize that medicines prescribed for depression and anxiety can also produce dependency problems.[1]

How Does Dependence Develop?

When the environment around any of the cells of your body changes, your body will try to compensate for it. If you move to a dry place, your kidneys will automatically increase their efficiency to conserve your body water. If you start taking a medicine that slows your heartbeat, your heart will begin to pump more blood with each beat.

These drugs produce their effects by changing the chemical environment around your brain cells. When this happens, your brain automatically adjusts itself to this changed environment by decreasing its own production of chemicals like the ones that the drug is supplying, and increasing its production of other chemicals. It may also grow new connections between one cell and another, and other connections may die back in response to this new milieu.[2] As time goes on, the drug-induced situation becomes the new norm for your brain.

As your brain adjusts itself to the presence of the medicine you are taking, the relief you gained from your depression or anxiety may begin to feel less complete than before. This may cause you to conclude that your depression or anxiety is returning or worsening. This is why patients who begin on relatively low dosages of antidepressants end up having their dosages increased. Sometimes additional medicines are prescribed to help overcome this loss of effectiveness, or "poop-out."

What Happens in Withdrawal?

If you suddenly stop taking your medicine, your brain will conclude that your newly nonmedicated state is abnormal and will try to compensate for it. You will experience unpleasant withdrawal symptoms until your brain adjusts itself to its new environment. These withdrawal symptoms will end when your brain has fully adjusted itself to the medicine's absence. This process is the same whether the drug you are taking is morphine, a pain pill, a tranquilizer or a sleeping pill, methamphetamine, cocaine, or an antidepressant. This is why words such as *dependence* and *withdrawal* are appropriate for describing the effects these drugs can have on the body.

Generally speaking, the most uncomfortable symptoms you will experience when you suddenly stop taking your medicine will be the same ones that led you to begin taking them in the first place. So if you are taking tranquilizers or antidepressants for anxiety, you will become anxious when you stop using the medication. If you are taking sleeping pills, you will have insomnia without them. If you are taking antidepressants for depression, you will become depressed and anxious if they are suddenly removed from your system.

It is important to understand that a woman who is dependent upon a drug is not necessarily trying to get "high" when she wants to keep on taking it, although this is certainly a factor in street drug addiction. But a desire to avoid these unpleasant symptoms is a powerful motivator toward continuing on medicines you have become dependent upon.

Doctors have known since the 1960s that dependence upon tranquilizers and sleeping pills can develop from continued usage, so they have no difficulty recognizing when this problem occurs. The symptoms that develop when the medicines are stopped are identified as withdrawal. But the antidepressants currently in use for anxiety and depression have not been around as long, and the drug literature often uses words such as *discontinuation syndrome* rather than *withdrawal* to describe what happens when a dependent person stops taking the medicine. This can lead to confusion about what is actually happening to you. For this reason, we have placed warnings throughout this book reminding you not to abruptly stop taking your medicines, and to have your doctor supervise your withdrawal from them.[3]

ANTIDEPRESSANT-INDUCED VIOLENCE AND SUICIDE

Although antidepressant-induced violence and suicide are problems that occur with just one class of psychiatric drugs, the antidepressants, we believe this is such a serious problem that we want to highlight it here rather than just mentioning it among the side effects antidepressants can produce.

Dr. Joseph Glenmullen of Harvard University Medical School links the occurrence of violence and suicide to side effects caused by antidepressants.[4] He explains that antidepressants can cause insomnia due to their stimulating effects. Anxiety is another common side effect, which can rise to the level of panic attacks in some women. Akathisia is a serious adverse reaction, a very unpleasant sensation of inner restlessness that has been described as feeling "squirmy," "like I want to jump out of my skin," or, in severe cases, "like I'm going to explode." It can also manifest itself as an agonizing sense of mental turmoil. Antidepressants can also trigger mania, irritability, hostility, impulsivity, paranoia, and psychosis.

It's not hard to see how these side effects could lead to violence or suicide, particularly in someone who did not understand that it was the medicine that was making her feel like this. Dr. Glenmullen points out that all of these side effects are linked:

> Anxiety can cause insomnia. Conversely, insomnia can make people anxious. Both anxiety and insomnia can be manifestations of akathisia or manic-like reactions. . . . Anxiety, insomnia, akathisia and manic-like reactions, in turn, can lead to irritability, hostility and impulsivity.[5]

Many women experiencing side effects such as these have concluded that they are going crazy. If you believed you were getting worse, not better, and feared you would never get better, you could be tempted to commit suicide. Some women even attempt suicide impulsively, without thinking the decision through. Laura recalls that this is what she experienced on the terrible night she described in her story at the beginning of this book. Dr. Glenmullen points out,

> In women in particular, antidepressant-induced suicidality is often much more violent than the suicidality seen in depression. Depressed women typically attempt suicide by overdosing rather than more violent means. But with antidepressant-induced suicidality, women typically attempt or commit suicide by unusually violent means: mutilating themselves with knives, hanging themselves, shooting themselves, or jumping off buildings (emphasis added).[6]

Dr. David Healy describes a study he designed in which healthy volunteers who were also health-care professionals took antidepressants and kept a record of their reactions to the medicines.[7] Chillingly, some of these healthy professionals experienced disturbing personality changes, vivid dreams of violent suicide, paranoia, and impulses to kill themselves using violent means. One woman got out of her car at midnight to pick a fight with a group of young men she didn't know because she thought they had insulted her, a choice that could have led her to being assaulted or even murdered. The most troubling aspect of this study is the long-term effect that the medicines had upon the volunteers' self-image, which persisted long after the medicines were stopped. Dr. Healy comments,

> The injury we had done both women was greater than these escapes [from suicide] suggested. Both remained disturbed several months later; both seriously questioned the stability of their personalities. At first this struck me as ludicrous. But we had great difficulty persuading them that it had been the drug—and only the drug. Their view of themselves had been shaken.[8]

Laura also found that her confidence in herself as a person who was competent to help others was completely destroyed by her experience on psychiatric medicines. It took her a long time to understand her struggles for what they really were. Yet she was the fortunate one—her brother Bill did not survive his suicidal thoughts.

As you can see, dependence and withdrawal can have serious consequences. When it comes to taking or stopping antidepressants, we hope that you will make your decisions very carefully, and always with the supervision of your doctor.

SIDE EFFECTS OF EACH DRUG CLASS

Let's now consider the general side effects that are associated with the various groups of psychiatric drugs: Stimulants and antidepressants, tranquilizers and sleeping pills, mood stabilizing medicines, and antipsychotic medicines. What follows is intended to serve as a very general overview and will not address every possible side effect for each individual drug. For more information on the specific side effects associated with your medicine, ask your doctor or pharmacist, or look up the medication in the most current *Physician's Desk Reference* (PDR).[9]

STIMULANTS AND ANTIDEPRESSANTS

We are placing these two groups of drugs together because their side effect profiles are very similar. Stimulants[10] have been prescribed to children diagnosed with Attention-Deficit Hyperactivity Disorder (ADHD) for many years.[11] More recently they have been prescribed to adults in increasing numbers for what is called Adult ADHD, and also for severe depression. These drugs are chemically related to the illegal stimulants cocaine and methamphetamine ("crystal meth"). Doctors have known since the 1960s that stimulants can produce dependence.

Antidepressants[12] are chemically related to stimulants and produce similar effects. They were initially developed as non-habit-forming stimulant drugs, although experience with them has shown that they also can produce dependence, as previously described. Antidepressants are prescribed for depression and anxiety. Although, as we mentioned in the section on suicide, antidepressants can produce anxiety as a side effect, they are prescribed at lower doses to *treat* anxiety.

The most serious risks of stimulant medicines, whether they are illegal drugs such as cocaine and "crystal" or prescription stimulants, are seizures, mania, and psychosis. They can also produce and worsen tics (frequent muscle spasms). Probably the most common effect of stimulants is loss of appetite, which is why these drugs were first sold as diet pills in the 1950s. Stimulants commonly cause nervousness, insomnia, irritability, and aggressiveness. They can also stunt the growth of children.

Stimulants can elevate your blood pressure and heart rate, and have been associated with heart and liver failure. The FDA very recently received, from an advisory panel that studied stimulant use in ADHD, a recommendation that the same "black box" warnings recently added to packages of antidepressants be added to the packages of certain stimulants prescribed for ADHD. That's because of the risk of cardiac side effects, which in some cases have resulted in deaths.[13]

Antidepressants, like stimulants, can produce seizures, mania, and psychosis. We think that the recent increase in the diagnosis of Bipolar II may be due to antidepressant-induced mania and manic-like reactions. Drug company literature speaks of antidepressants "activating" a latent bipolar disorder—in other words, bringing out a disease that was already there. But Dr. Glenmullen reminds us,

> When people take so much cocaine that they have manic-like reactions and end up in an emergency room, they are diagnosed with cocaine toxicity. When people have manic-like reactions to steroids, they are diagnosed with steroid toxicity. Yet when people have the same type of reactions to antidepressants, they are diagnosed with so-called "underlying bipolar disorder."[14]

The FDA has also warned physicians that manic-like reactions such as agitation, insomnia, irritability, hostility, impulsivity, and akathisia (severe restlessness), as well as anxiety and panic attacks, are associated with the use of antidepressants.[15]

Extrapyramidal symptoms (EPS) are potentially very serious adverse reactions to these medicines.[16] These include akathisia (an agonizing inner restlessness), dyskinesia (involuntary movements of the body), dystonia (involuntary muscle spasms), and drug-induced Parkinson's syndrome. Some doctors think that akathisia may be behind the irritability, aggression, and suicidal thoughts that some people develop on these medicines. Tardive dyskinesia (TD), a dreaded side effect, produces involuntary movements that may become permanent. There is no cure for TD, although it sometimes can decrease or go away on its own, over time.

Appetite is often poor at the beginning of antidepressant treatment, and you might even lose weight initially, but later on, weight gains of twenty pounds or more are common. Loss of sexual drive is also very common.

Antidepressants have also been implicated in birth defects, and babies born to women who take antidepressants may experience drug withdrawal after they are born.[17] The FDA recently released a formal health advisory to physicians about the risk of serious birth defects in the children of women taking Paxil.[18] Another recent study found withdrawal symptoms in one-third of infants born to women who were taking antidepressants at the time of delivery.[19] If you are pregnant or might become pregnant, we believe you should not take these medicines.

Once again, we want to emphasize that these drugs can *cause* anxiety, depression, and insomnia, even though they are also prescribed to *treat* these very problems.

Tranquilizers and Sleeping Pills

We place tranquilizers[20] and sleeping pills[21] together because they also are closely related from a chemical standpoint. Generally speaking, the difference between tranquilizers and sleeping pills is the dosages at which they are prescribed. Less of a tranquilizer will render a woman relaxed, but awake, and more will put her to sleep.

You probably already know that tranquilizers and sleeping pills can produce dependence. They also can produce the same kinds of liver problems that alcohol can produce if they are taken at high enough doses for a long enough period of time. All relaxants—whether alcohol, street drugs, tranquilizers, or sleeping pills—can also produce anxiety and depression, as described earlier in chapter 2.

If you have been in the hospital on account of suicidal thoughts, you may have received sleeping pills or tranquilizers during your stay. If you did, it is important for you to understand that you should stop taking them at the earliest possible opportunity after the crisis is over, because the ongoing use of these drugs is a common cause of therapeutic tail-chasing. The depression and anxiety they can produce can lead your doctor to prescribe more antidepressant medicine than you might otherwise need.

Other common side effects associated with use of these medicines are drowsiness, dizziness, confusion, unsteadiness, coordination problems, weakness, memory problems, and sometimes even amnesia that lasts a brief while.

MOOD-STABILIZING MEDICINES

There are two basic types of mood-stabilizing medicines: lithium (a naturally occurring elemental salt) and anticonvulsants (medicines that are also used to treat epilepsy). Lithium[22] can produce all of the extrapyramidal symptoms (EPS) described in the section on antidepressants. People who take lithium commonly complain of shaking, confusion, mental slowing, and memory problems. Serious kidney, heart, and thyroid problems have been associated with lithium use. It can also cause hair loss, weight gain, and acne.

The toxic level of lithium is nearly the same as the therapeutic level. This means that women can experience toxic effects even when their blood levels are within the proper range. Those who take lithium have frequent blood tests taken to check their lithium levels, but there is no guarantee that if the blood level is correct, there will be no toxicity. Lithium toxicity, which is a dangerous condition in which the blood's lithium level is too high, can produce kidney damage, coma, and brain damage.

Anticonvulsants[23] are commonly used to treat unstable moods. Some of them can cause life-threatening liver damage and pancreatitis, low blood platelet levels (platelets are what help our blood to clot), and high blood ammonia levels. High blood ammonia levels can lead to coma and death. Tegretol can cause your bone marrow to stop making blood cells. Lamictal can produce two potentially fatal diseases accompanied by rare skin rashes. Depakote is known to produce birth defects in pregnant women, so you should not take it under any circumstances if it is possible that you could become pregnant. Nausea, sleepiness, dizziness, and weakness are also frequent side effects of the anticonvulsants.

Antipsychotic Medicines

Antipsychotic drugs are used to treat "crazy" thoughts and behavior. There are two basic groups of antipsychotic drugs: The older drugs produce a very high rate of EPS, as described in the section on antidepressants.[24] They are rarely used anymore, but have been largely replaced by newer drugs such as Zyprexa and Risperdal.

The most serious side effect of antipsychotic medicines is tardive dyskinesia (TD). A person with TD can develop permanent involuntary movements, particularly of the face and neck. These movements can include uncontrollable sticking out the tongue and grimacing. The older antipsychotic drugs have resulted in high rates of TD after long-term use. As we mentioned in the section on antidepressants, TD can become permanent, and there is no known cure.

The new antipsychotic medicines have not been in use long enough for us to know their propensity to produce TD. Those who have had episodes of EPS are at higher risk for TD, and the newer antipsychotics produce less EPS. So with these newer drugs, the risk for TD, over time, will probably be lower than with the older ones.

One significant problem with the newer antipsychotic drugs is uncontrolled and sometimes massive weight gain over time. This weight gain increases the risk of diabetes in those who take these drugs. Another serious side effect is neuroleptic malignant syndrome (NMS). This is a rare complication that can lead to death.

Other common side effects include sleepiness, low blood pressure, fainting, and seizures. Women may discover that their menstrual periods have ceased due to a hormone that these medicines may elevate. Liver damage and an inability to tolerate hot weather can occur.

A WARNING FOR WOMEN ON ANTIPSYCHOTICS AND MOOD STABILIZERS

Even though the side effects that can occur with mood-stabilizing and antipsychotic medicines are frightening, these drugs can be lifesaving for women who are truly psychotic or manic. We encourage you to carefully read chapter 8 before making a decision about your continued use of antipsychotic medicines. A woman who has never been psychotic or manic may be given these medicines for mood swings (as described in chapter 7) or for uncontrolled behavior (as mentioned in chapter 8). These medicines are also given to treat psychotic or manic-like side effects of stimulant or antidepressant treatment. While you may be willing to accept the risk of such serious side effects if the medicine is needed treat true psychosis or mania, these medicines should not be used to help problems that would respond just as well to careful, medically supervised discontinuation of antidepressants and competent biblical counseling.

AND DON'T FORGET . . .

We want to remind you one more time that if you decide that you want to stop taking any psychiatric medicine, you should do so under the supervision of a doctor. Although dependence has not been attributed to mood-stabilizing and antipsychotic medicines, abrupt withdrawal of medicines that are stabilizing a true psychosis or mania could lead to a relapse. Dependence will probably begin to develop if you use a stimulant, antidepressant, tranquilizer, and sleeping pill treatment for more than a couple of weeks.

HOW TO
TALK WITH
YOUR DOCTOR

IF YOU ARE already taking psychiatric medicines, or if your doctor wants you to start taking them, you may be wondering how to discuss with him what you have learned in this book. We believe that every woman, whether she is already taking these medicines or considering them, needs to ask her doctor specific questions about why he or she thinks she needs these medicines and how long he anticipates that she will need to take them. We also believe she should ask him about any alternatives to medicine that are available. Another important question to ask is whether your doctor has had experience with prescribing psychiatric drugs as well as helping patients stop taking them. This appendix is intended to help you start a conversation with your doctor about these matters.

IF YOU HAVE NOT YET STARTED
TAKING PSYCHIATRIC MEDICINES

Women very often receive psychiatric medicines for the first time from their family doctors. Sometimes this is because they have mentioned to their doctor that they are experiencing stress or depression or anxiety, and his or her response is to offer a prescription for an antidepressant. Other times, a doctor concludes that a woman's pain problem is "really" depression, or that she "must" be depressed because she has a serious medical condition. When Laura began breast cancer treatment some years ago, she was offered an antidepressant without ever complaining of feeling depressed!

We have met women who started taking an antidepressant because their doctor prescribed it and they concluded that they must need it or she wouldn't have offered it to them. But their doctor may not have intended to suggest that this was the only alternative, or that the medicine was a necessary treatment. It never hurts to ask questions and to clarify exactly what your doctor has in mind when she offers you a medicine that may change your emotional responses.

If your doctor says she wants you to take an antidepressant as a treatment for a medical condition, we suggest you ask which of your symptoms the doctor expects the medicine to improve, and specifically how the medicine will accomplish this. What you want to learn is whether your doctor is offering you the medicine as a treatment for a disease, or to help you feel better emotionally. This distinction is important because you will want to take any medicine your doctor says is *necessary*, but you might choose *not* to take a medicine if you understood that it was intended for your feelings and that taking it was *optional*.

If your doctor wants to prescribe a medicine to make you feel better, ask her to clarify whether medicine is *required* for your particular problem, or if she thinks that you could improve through counseling or making adjustments in your lifestyle, such as the ones we have mentioned in this book. In our experience, doctors often offer medicines when they think this is what their patient wants, but they may also know about other more commonsense solutions that are just as good, or even better. So it is important for you to find out what your doctor really believes will be the most helpful for you.

We also suggest you ask your doctor whether she thinks the benefits of taking the medicine outweigh the risks of serious side effects such as dependency and violent or suicidal thoughts. You will definitely want to find out how long she thinks you will need to take the medicine, and what plan she has for helping you to deal with any withdrawal symptoms you might experience when you stop taking it.

If you do choose to take psychiatric medicines, they should be prescribed and monitored by a psychiatrist because of the risks of serious side effects and dependency. We suggest that if you are seeing a psychologist (a Ph.D. who is not licensed to practice medicine) or other secular counselor who wants you to go on medicine, you should ask for the second opinion of a psychiatrist (a medical doctor who specializes in prescribing these medicines) rather than going to your family doctor for your prescription. We also encourage you to consider changing your secular psychologist or counselor for a biblical counselor who can help you according to the principles in this book. (You can find a referral to a biblical counselor online at www.nanc.org, or perhaps through your church.)

We have noticed a trend in some psychiatric offices toward delegating medicine prescription or monitoring to nurse practitioners or physician's assistants. In a few states, even psychologists are permitted to prescribe psychiatric drugs on the basis of having taken a very limited psychiatric prescription course. These psychologists have not had as much medical training as nurses or physician's assistants, yet they are allowed to prescribe medicines without even the *indirect* physician supervision that the law requires for nurses and physician's assistants. We believe that if you are going to be taking potentially dangerous drugs, it ought to be under the *direct* supervision of a physician specialist. We also recommend that you receive concurrent counseling from a Bible-believing counselor, and that you take the medicines for the shortest time possible.

IF YOU ALREADY TAKE PSYCHIATRIC MEDICINES

If, as so often happens, you were given an antidepressant some months or years ago and your family doctor simply refills your prescription when you run out of it without asking questions, you and he may both be assuming that the other person would bring up the subject if the medicine were not still needed. If this is the case, you might be surprised at what your doctor might say if you asked him if he thinks you still need to be on the medicine. We suggest you go ahead and ask, because starting this kind of conversation may be the first step toward developing a new and medicine-free treatment plan. Also, if you are wondering whether you might be dependent on your medicines or whether you might experience withdrawal symptoms if you stopped taking them, we suggest you ask your doctor about this issue.

If you have already tried to stop taking your antidepressant and your bad feelings have returned, you may have been told by your doctor that this means you have a disease and will need to take your antidepressant indefinitely. In this case, we suggest that you ask him if it is possible that you have experienced antidepressant withdrawal symptoms rather than a relapse of your depression. Similarly, if you have had your dosage of antidepressant increased since you first started taking it, or if you have developed additional symptoms and had another drug added, we believe you should ask your doctor whether your bad feelings might actually be due to side effects or drug dependency. We also recommend that you consider getting a second opinion, particularly if the doctor who has been prescribing these medicines to you is not a psychiatric specialist.

If you are currently taking several medicines, we suggest you ask your doctor if he thinks you could do well on fewer of them. Simplifying a drug regimen often produces remarkable improvement. In addition, if you can get down to taking just one medicine, it will be much easier to stop altogether when you and your doctor agree that you are ready to try this.

If you have been on psychiatric medicines for longer than a few months, we recommend you ask your doctor how much longer he thinks you should remain on the medicines. If he says you should be on them for the rest of your life, he should give you a good reason— such as the fact you have a permanent psychosis or Alzheimer's disease.

If he tells you that your "disease" of depression will require lifelong treatment, we suggest that you consider getting a second opinion.

In many cases we have found that asking for a second opinion is not necessary because many doctors are very receptive to a request to decrease or stop taking psychiatric medicines. You may find your doctor will be especially willing to try stopping your medicines if you have been in counseling and have addressed the underlying causes of the feelings that led to your receiving them in the first place. If your doctor tells you he doesn't think you are ready to stop taking your medicines, we encourage you to ask him what you could do to become ready. Often a doctor will suggest you decrease your alcohol intake, stop taking medicines that may have a depressant effect (such as sleeping pills), or go on a weight-loss program and keep more regular hours.

If you find you do need a second opinion, you should ask the second doctor if there is any reason you could not do well without medicines in the future, and how he would help you to work toward that goal if you continue to see him. And if you have not been receiving biblical counseling up to this point, this would be a great time to start! We have seen many women do well when they begin to see a new doctor who simplifies their drug regimen or is willing to consider slowly taking them off their medicines altogether, especially when they are receiving biblical counseling at the same time.

Because many family doctors do not have much experience with discontinuing psychiatric medicines, you may want to ask if you can be referred to a psychiatrist. You may find that your family doctor will be quick to admit he does not have a lot of experience in medicine withdrawal, and that he would be happy to refer you to a specialist.

We trust these suggestions will help you to begin talking with your doctor and to gain the information you need to make the choice that is right for you. May the Lord give you wisdom and guide you as you make these important decisions about your health and future!

RESOURCES
FOR
FURTHER STUDY

BIBLICAL BOOKS ON SPECIFIC TOPICS

Alcohol and drug abuse:

Edward T. Welch, *Addictions: A Banquet in the Grave: Finding Hope in the Power of the Gospel* (Phillipsburg, NJ: P & R Publishing, 2001).

Anorexia, bulimia, overeating:

Elyse Fitzpatrick, *Love to Eat, Hate to Eat* (Eugene, OR: Harvest House, 1999).

Elyse Fitzpatrick, *Uncommon Vessels* (Stanley, NC: Timeless Texts, 1990).

Biblical counseling:

Elyse Fitzpatrick and Carol Cornish, gen. eds., *Women Helping Women: A Biblical Guide to the Major Issues Women Face* (Eugene, OR: Harvest House, 1997).

David Powlison, *Seeing with New Eyes: Counseling the Human Condition Through the Lens of Scripture* (Phillipsburg, NJ: P & R Publishing, 2003).

Paul David Tripp, *Instruments in the Redeemer's Hands* (Phillipsburg, NJ: P & R Publishing, 2002).

Communication:

Paul Tripp, *War of Words* (Phillipsburg, NJ: P & R Publishing, 2000).

Conflict:

Tara Klena Barthel and Judy Dabler, *Peacemaking Women* (Grand Rapids: Baker, 2005).
Ken Sande, *PeaceMaker,* 3rd ed. (Grand Rapids: Baker, 2004).
Ken Sande, *Peacemaking in Families* (Wheaton: Tyndale House, 2002).

Depression:

Wayne Mack, *Down but Not Out: How to Get Up When Life Knocks You Down* (Phillipsburg, NJ: P & R Publishing, 2005).
Edward T. Welch, *Depression: A Stubborn Darkness* (Winston-Salem, NC: Punch Press, 2004).

Fear:

Elyse Fitzpatrick, *Overcoming Fear, Worry, and Anxiety* (Eugene, OR: Harvest House, 2001).
Wayne Mack and Joshua Mack, *The Fear Factor: What Satan Doesn't Want You to Know* (Tulsa: Hensley Publishing, 2003).
Edward T. Welch, *When People Are Big and God Is Small* (Phillipsburg, NJ: P & R Publishing, 1997).

Idolatry:

Elyse Fitzpatrick, *Idols of the Heart: Learning to Long for God Alone* (Phillipsburg, NJ: P & R Publishing, 2001).

Pain:

Dr. James Halla, *Pain, the Plight of Fallen Man* (Stanley, NC: Timeless Texts, 2002).

Spousal abuse:

Robert B. Needham and Debra S. Pryde, *What Do You Do When You're Abused by Your Husband?* (Long Beach, CA: Growth Publications, 2000).

Suffering:

Elisabeth Elliot, *A Path Through Suffering: Discovering the Relationship Between God's Mercy and Our Pain* (Ann Arbor, MI: Servant Publications, 1990).

Joni Eareckson Tada and Steve Estes, *When God Weeps: Why Our Sufferings Matter to the Almighty* (Grand Rapids: Zondervan, 1997).

Resources for Changing Lives produces a number of very helpful pamphlets that will help you think biblically about your troubling emotions. You can find these pamphlets at www.ccef.org.

The National Association of Nouthetic Counselors (NANC) is a fellowship of pastors and laypeople who have banded together to promote counseling that uses the Bible to help people change. NANC is a certifying and referral organization that can refer you to a certified biblical counselor in your area. We highly recommend that you consider working with a counselor who has been trained through and certified by NANC. You can contact NANC for a referral to a biblical counselor at www.nanc.org, or you can call their offices at (317) 337-9100.

Secular Books About Psychotropic Medicines:

David Healy, *Let Them Eat Prozac: The Unhealthy Relationship Between the Pharmaceutical Industry and Depression* (New York: New York University Press, 2004).

Joseph Glenmullen, M.D., *The Antidepressant Solution: A Step-by-Step Guide to Safely Overcoming Antidepressant Withdrawal, Dependence, and "Addiction"* (New York: Free Press, 2005).

The PDR Pocket Guide to Prescription Drugs (New York: Pocket Books, 2003).

NOTES

CHAPTER 1: WHAT'S WRONG WITH ME?

1. Some Christians believe we are made up of two parts (body and soul or spirit), and others teach we have three parts (body, soul, and spirit). The authors believe in the two-part view, which is why we have presented the material as we have, but the three-part view is also consistent with orthodox, biblical Christianity. Some of the passages that speak of this dual (or triple) nature of humanity are Psalm 26:2; 1 Chronicles 28:9; Jeremiah 17:10; 20:12; Psalm 139:14; Lamentations 3:20; 3 John 1:2; Deuteronomy 4:9; 7:17; Proverbs 2:10; Ephesians 6:6; 1 Thessalonians 5:23; Hebrews 4:12.

2. Sometimes the Bible uses the word *mind* to refer to the inner person when it describes our thoughts, *will* to refer to the inner person when it talks about choices, and various words for *feelings* when it refers to emotions. Because of this, some people like to divide the inner person into three additional subdivisions, consisting of the mind, will, and emotions. We believe it is easier simply to call the inner person the *mind* when discussing thinking, the *will* when discussing choosing, and the *heart* when referring to emotions. We will follow this convention throughout the book.

3. *The Spirit of the Reformation Study Bible* (Grand Rapids: Zondervan, 2003), 976, describes the inner person this way in its notes on the book of Proverbs:

   In biblical anthropology the heart controls the body (14:13), including its facial expressions (15:13), the tongue (12:23; 15:28) and all its other members (4:23–27; 6:18). The Scriptures also attribute to the heart control over physiological functions (see 17:3; 24:12) and mention it as the seat of emotional experience (see 12:25; 14:10, 30; 15:15; 17:3; 24:12). The heart thinks, reflects and ponders (24:2). The heart plans (6:14,18; 16:9) and functions as the inner forum where decisions are made. The heart also accepts and trusts in the religious sphere (3:5). Closely related to its pious function is its ethical activity (see 6:25; 15:14; 23:17; 15:7; 17:16, 20; 19:3; 24:2; 26:23–25). This direction or bent of the heart determines its directions and, in turn, the person's actions (cf. Ex. 14:5; 35:21; Nu. 32:9; 1Ki. 12:27; 18:37). Since the heart is the source of an individual's emotional, intellectual, religious and moral activity, it must be safeguarded above all things ([Proverbs] 4:23). Paradoxically, although the eyes and ears are gates to the heart (4:20–23), the heart decides what they will hear and see (4:23–26).

4. Edward T. Welch, *Blame It on the Brain* (Phillipsburg, N.J.: P & R Publishing, 1998), 48.

5. The Bible often uses the word *mind* to refer to the part of our inner person (or heart) that thinks. Because the brain is a part of the physical body, not the inner person, *mind* is *not* another word for *brain.*

6. For reasons that are not well understood, some women do not improve at all on antidepressants. Others are only partially improved. This is known among psychiatrists as treatment-resistant depression. In addition, the fact that anti-depressants can lose effectiveness over time is well-known. We will be discussing this loss of effectiveness or "poop-out" further in chapter 2.

7. See, for example, Psalm 55:18; Philippians 2:12–13; 4:13, 19; 2 Corinthians 5:17; 9:8; 2 Peter 1:3.

CHAPTER 2: WILL MEDICINE HELP MY PAIN?

1. The classic work on this topic, by Norman Cousins, is *Anatomy of an Illness as Perceived by the Patient* (New York: Norton, 1979).

2. For further information on the problem of antidepressant dependency, see Joseph Glenmullen, M.D., *The Antidepressant Solution: A Step-by-Step Guide to Safely Overcoming Antidepressant Withdrawal, Dependence, and "Addiction"* (New York: Free Press, Simon & Schuster, 2005).

3. Dr. Joseph Glenmullen, *Prozac Backlash* (New York: Simon and Schuster, 2001), 91. Glenmullen, in citing these figures, refers to M. Fava, S. M. Rappe, J. A. Pava, A. A. Nierenberg, J. E. Alpert, and J. F. Rosenbaum, "Relapse in Patients on Long-Term Fluoxetine [Prozac] Treatment: Response to Increased Fluoxetine [Prozac] Dose," *Journal of Clinical Psychiatry* 56 (1995): 52–55.

4. A recent book that presents a twenty-five-year history of the connection of increased suicide with antidepressant use is psychiatrist David Healy's *Let Them Eat Prozac* (New York: New York University Press, 2004).

5. Ibid., 64–66, 81–84, 90–93.

6. Ibid., xiv.

7. Ibid., 263–66.

8. For more information on the issue of brain rewiring, see Glenmullen, *Prozac Backlash*, 57–59, 94–100.

9. A recent book that presents an excellent summary of neuroplastic research is psychiatrist Jeffrey Schwartz's *The Mind and the Brain* (New York: Regan Books, 2002). Although we find it interesting that a secular Buddhist psychiatrist agrees with us about the existence of the inner person, we do not agree with his attempts to explain the presence of the inner person, which he refers to as "mental force" apart from faith in a Creator God. But we recommend the book for those interested in learning more about how the way we think and

what we practice changes our brain *without medicines*.

10. For example, see the self-help book by psychiatrist Jeffrey Schwartz, *Brain Lock* (New York: Regan Books, 1996), which demonstrates that as people with obsessive-compulsive disorder resist their disturbing thoughts, their functional brain imaging changes in a more normal direction. Please note that we are not recommending Dr. Schwartz's method of changing thoughts. We are just offering his research observations as encouraging evidence that changing the thoughts of your inner person can change the function of your bodily organ, the brain. For a biblical method for changing thoughts, see chapter 6 in this book.

11. In studies that compare counseling with medicine as a means of treatment, the studies that find medicine to be the superior form of treatment generally show a relatively small percentage difference between those helped by counseling interventions and those helped by medicines. We are not aware of any study showing that counseling interventions are ineffective, or of any study showing that medicines are strongly superior to a counseling approach. See Robert Rubeis et. al., "Medications vs. Cognitive Behavior Therapy for Severely Depressed Outpatients: A Meta-Analysis of Four Randomized Comparisons," *American Journal of Psychiatry* 156 (1999): 1007–13, as one example of a study that did not show that medications were superior to counseling.

12. We do not want to suggest that our beliefs should be determined by whether or not secular research agrees with the teachings of God's Word. But those who might worry about whether biblical counseling is an "unscientific" approach to emotional pain can be reassured by knowing that secular science seems to affirm the teachings of this book.

CHAPTER 3: LORD, WHY DO YOU LET ME HURT?

1. Richard Baxter, *A Christian Directory* (Morgan, Penn.: Soli Deo Gloria Publications, 1996), 75.

2. The Shorter Catechism, Q. 1, *The Westminster Standards* (Suwanee, Ga.: Great Commission Publications, 1997), 71.

3. J. I. Packer, *Growing in Christ* (Wheaton: Crossway Books), 1994, electronic edition, copyright 1996.

4. It is reasonable to ask whether it's right for God to be focused on His own glory. After all, isn't that cosmically selfish of Him? First, it's proper for God to seek His own glory because He is so wonderful that for Him to seek after or desire anything else would be treachery and idolatry. It's right for Him to seek after His own honor because He deserves all honor. When we see the differences between Himself and us, and note how kind and merciful He's been to us, we worship Him, and it's only then that we begin to experience the real joy He's longing for us to know.

5. See Joni Eareckson Tada, *When God Weeps* (Grand Rapids: Zondervan, 1997), and *The God I Love: A Lifetime of Walking with Jesus* (Grand Rapids: Zondervan, 2004); see Corrie ten Boom, *The Hiding Place* (New York: Bantam, 1981).

6. C. S. Lewis, *The Problem of Pain* (New York: Macmillan, 1977), 91.

7. For more on this see Elyse Fitzpatrick, *Idols of the Heart: Learning to Long for God Alone* (Phillipsburg, N.J.: P & R Publishing, 2001).

CHAPTER 4: LORD, WHY DID YOU HURT YOUR SON?

1. We're not saying that the Jews and Romans weren't responsible in any way for the death of Christ. Rather, we're saying that although they were responsible for their sinful desires and actions, God was ruling sovereignly over them in order to accomplish His good purposes. Acts 2:22–23 makes this clear: "Men of Israel, listen to these words: Jesus the Nazarene, a man attested to you by God with miracles and wonders and signs which God performed through Him in your midst, just as you yourselves know—this Man, delivered over by the predetermined plan and foreknowledge of God, you nailed to a cross by the hands of godless men and put Him to death." Godless men certainly did "mean it for evil," but God meant it for good and ruled over all of what happened.

2. Other verses that speak of God's work of justifying and adopting us are Matthew 20:28; Romans 3:24–26; 4:25; 5:6–10,15–21; 8:15–17; 1 Corinthians 15:3; 2 Corinthians 5:21; Hebrews 10:10, 14; 1 Peter 3:18.

3. James Strong, *Enhanced Strong's Lexicon,* G5485 (Ontario: Woodside Bible Fellowship, 1996).

4. Jerry Bridges, *Transforming Grace: Living Confidently in God's Unfailing Love*, A Discussion Guide Based on the Book (Colorado Springs: NavPress, 1991), 67.

5. *Vine's Expository Dictionary of Biblical Words,* s.v. "buffet" (Nashville: Thomas Nelson Publishers, 1985).

6. *Jamieson, Fausset, and Brown Commentary*, s.v. Colossians 1:24, electronic database, copyright 1997 by Biblesoft.

7. Mother Teresa is quoted as saying, "In comparison to the glories of heaven, the most miserable life here on earth will seem like one night spent in an inconvenient motel." As cited in Edward T. Welch, "Exalting Pain? Ignoring Pain? What Do We Do with Suffering?" *Journal of Biblical Counseling* 12, no. 3 (Spring 1994): 15.

CHAPTER 5: DEPRESSION: AN OPPORTUNITY IN DISGUISE

1. For more information on withdrawal from any of the antidepressants, see Joseph Glenmullen, M.D., *The Antidepressant Solution: A Step-by-Step Guide to Safely Overcoming Antidepressant Withdrawal, Dependence, and "Addiction"* (New York: Free Press, Simon & Schuster, 2005).

2. If you're away from home or don't know any godly women you can talk to, we encourage you to call a nearby Bible-teaching church and ask for help. If you don't know what kind of church to call, then you might ask the pastor (or a leader) the following questions: Do you believe that the Bible is the inerrant

and sufficient Word of God? Do you believe that Jesus Christ was sent to pay the full penalty for sin and that His death, burial, and resurrection is sufficient to purchase full redemption for those who believe in Him? Do you believe that salvation is by faith alone, in Christ alone, and by grace alone? Do you believe that the Bible has all the answers for Christians who desire to live a godly life? These questions will let you know whether you have found a Bible-believing church and whether you'll be able to find help there. If the answer to any of these questions is no, then try again with another congregation. We trust that the Lord will guide you to real help, since He's commissioned the church for just this kind of need.

3. For a broader understanding of this, see Elyse Fitzpatrick, *Idols of the Heart: Learning to Long for God Alone* (Phillipsburg, N.J.: P & R Publishing, 2001).
4. An excellent book on the assurance of God's love even though we fail is Peter Dathenus's *The Pearl of Christian Comfort* (Grand Rapids: Reformation Heritage Books, 1997).
5. K. Sempangi, *A Distant Grief* (Ventura, Calif.: Regal, 1979), 179, as cited in Edward T. Welch, *Depression: A Stubborn Darkness* (Winston-Salem, N.C.: Punch Press, 2004), 48.
6. Thanks to Dr. Jay Adams for developing the idea of the spiral of depression.
7. And if you would like to read more about biblical ways to deal with depression, a wonderful resource is Welch, *Depression*, 2004).

CHAPTER 6: CASTING ALL YOUR ANXIETY ON HIM

1. *Spurgeon's Encyclopedia of Sermons,* "Our Needless Fears," a sermon delivered on Thursday evening, June 11, 1874, by C. H. Spurgeon at the Metropolitan Tabernacle, Newington (emphasis added), electronic database, copyright 1997 by Biblesoft.
2. *Matthew Henry's Commentary on the Whole Bible,* New Modern Edition, electronic database, copyright 1991 by Hendrickson Publishers.
3. For more information on OCD, see Michael R. Emlet, *OCD: Freedom for the Obsessive-Compulsive* (Phillipsburg, N.J.: P & R Publishing, 2004).
4. For more information on self-injury, see Edward T. Welch, *Self-Injury: When Pain Feels Good* (Phillipsburg, N.J.: P & R Publishing, 2004).
5. Excerpted from Elyse Fitzpatrick, *Overcoming Fear, Worry, and Anxiety: Becoming a Woman of Faith and Confidence* (Eugene, Ore.: Harvest House, 2001), 120–21.
6. Edward T. Welch, *When People Are Big and God Is Small* (Phillipsburg, N.J.: P & R Publishing, 1997), 97–98.

CHAPTER 7: UNDERSTANDING YOUR OUT-OF-CONTROL MOODS

1. John Calvin, *Institutes of the Christian Religion*, ed. John T. McNeill, vol. 1 (Philadelphia: Westminster, 1960), 108. The metaphor of idolatry in this

chapter and "treasure" in the previous chapters are analagous.

2. For more information on heart idolatry, see Elyse Fitzpatrick, *Idols of the Heart: Learning to Long for God Alone* (Phillipsburg, N.J.: P & R Publishing, 2001).

3. John Flavel, *Keeping the Heart: A Puritan's View of How to Maintain Your Love for God* (Fearn, Great Britain: Christian Focus, 1999), 8–9.

4. Ibid., 13.

5. David Powlison, *Stress: Peace Amid Pressure* (Phillipsburg, N.J.: P & R Publishing, 2004), 13–14.

6. C. S. Lewis, *The Screwtape Letters* (New York: Macmillan, 1982), 79.

7. For extra help with the problem of overeating, see Elyse Fitzpatrick, *Love to Eat, Hate to Eat* (Eugene, Ore.: Harvest House, 1999). For extra help with the problem of substance abuse, see Edward T. Welch, *Addictions: A Banquet in the Grave* (Phillipsburg, N.J.: P & R Publishing, 2001).

CHAPTER 8: WHAT ABOUT COGNITIVE AND PERCEPTUAL PROBLEMS?

1. You can read the story of Phineas Gage at http://science-education.nih.gov /nihHTML/ose/snapshots/multimedia/ritn/Gage/Broken_brain1.html.

2. Jay E. Adams, *A Theology of Christian Counseling: More than Redemption* (Grand Rapids: Zondervan, 1979), 167–68.

3. Dr. Jay Adams says just because a mistake is related to an error in perception does not exclude the co-occurrence of faulty perception with deliberate deception on some point, or with "sinful practices, attitudes, beliefs." One can also be deceived by wrong doctrine, and "when a counselee *adopts* erroneous explanations of life or teachings, he is always responsible for doing so," no matter what other factors also may be involved. Adams concludes, "The matter is complex; there may be multiple possible causes for the same effect; or multiple-combined causes for it! Error, then, is always the result of sin (Adam's sin), but not always, in addition, the consequence of actual sin by the one in error. The matter is not simple" (*Theology of Christian Counseling*, 168).

4. Ibid.

5. For a first-person account of the course of recovery in TBI, see Cathy Crimmons, *Where Is the Mango Princess?: A Journey Back from Brain Injury* (New York: Vintage Books, 2000). Ms. Crimmons tells the story of her attorney husband's head injury and how it changed his personality and behavior. (Warning: This is not a Christian book, and some of the language is very profane. But the story this book tells is powerful, and for this reason it is worthy of reading.)

6. *Schizophrenia* is the term psychiatrists use to describe a particular type of psychotic disorder characterized by hallucinations and delusions. In the middle twentieth century it was widely believed that schizophrenia occurred as a consequence of unconscious conflicts or as a result of poor parental nurture. Dr.

Jay Adams correctly pointed out many years ago that this assessment was based upon an unbiblical worldview and therefore could not be true. His position was vindicated some years ago when scientists returned to their previous understanding of schizophrenia as a disease of the brain.

Dr. Adams has been widely quoted as saying that there is no such thing as schizophrenia. He has explained that he means that the term *schizophrenia* describes behavior rather than defining its cause, which is still unknown. The proliferation of the diagnosis of schizophrenia in the middle to late twentieth century was often a response to out-of-control behavior rather than a determination that there was evidence of true brain disease. Many women who were temporarily overwhelmed by emotional pain received this diagnosis during those years. Dr. Adams also points out that some people who receive this diagnosis later admit to having pretended to be crazy, for whatever reason. Because there is room for question about the accuracy of diagnoses of schizophrenia, we believe that any woman who has received this diagnosis should consult her doctor to see if she can try to withdraw from her medicine in order to determine whether she actually has a brain disease, or whether she carries that diagnosis because of a wrong assessment of a temporary emotional upset.

As explained in his book *A Theology of Christian Counseling*, Dr. Adams has always taught that biblical theology allows for a disease process that results in faulty perception, and that this faulty perception may be a mitigating factor in the behavioral disturbances seen in severe brain diseases. All this being said, we still believe *schizophrenia* is a useful term, if for no other reason than that most people use it, while we agree with Dr. Adams that it does not say anything about the true cause of the behaviors it describes.

7. Joni Eareckson Tada and Steve Estes, *When God Weeps: Why Our Sufferings Matter to the Almighty* (Grand Rapids: Zondervan, 1997), 108.

CHAPTER 9: ALL FOR THE GLORY OF GOD

1. This doesn't mean the blind man and his parents were sinless. It only means that his blindness was not a direct result of their sin. We all suffer the effects of the fall and our sinfulness, but our suffering doesn't necessarily correlate directly to specific sins. This, if nothing else, is what the book of Job teaches us.

2. *Vine's Expository Dictionary of Biblical Words*, s.v. "temperance," copyright 1985, Thomas Nelson.

3. Ibid., s.v. "godliness."

APPENDIX B

1. Dr. Joseph Glenmullen, a Harvard University psychiatrist, doesn't think the words *dependence* and *withdrawal* are too extreme to describe the difficulties associated with the discontinuation of these medicines. He has been warning about this problem for the last ten years, and uses these words in his recent

book *The Antidepressant Solution: A Step-by-Step Guide to Safely Overcoming Antidepressant Withdrawal, Dependence, and "Addiction"* (New York: Free Press, 2005). Dr. David Healy, psychiatrist and former secretary of the British Association for Psychopharmacology, agrees. See his recent book *Let Them Eat Prozac: The Unhealthy Relationship Between the Pharmaceutical Industry and Depression* (New York: New York University Press, 2004), 26–29, 270–72.

2. Dr. Joseph Glenmullen, *Prozac Backlash* (New York: Simon and Schuster, 2001), 94–105.

3. We suggest you read Glenmullen's *The Antidepressant Solution* (cited in end-note 1) before you discuss stopping your medicines with your doctor. You should show your doctor the recommendations this book makes before he decides how quickly you should go off of the medicines. If he is not familiar with this problem, ask him to refer you to a psychiatrist who has experience with supervising a patient's withdrawal from antidepressant dependence.

4. Glenmullen, *Antidepressant Solution*, 49–76.

5. Ibid., 72.

6. Ibid., 67.

7. Healy, *Let Them Eat Prozac*, 174–88.

8. Ibid., 187.

9. *Physician's Desk Reference* is published annually (Montvale, N.J.: Thompson PDR). Most libraries have a copy of this book, which contains encyclopedic listing of specific drug side effects.

10. These include Ritalin, Dexedrine, Concerta, and Adderal.

11. For more information on concerns about the use of psychiatric medicines in children, please see Elyse Fitzpatrick, Jim Newheiser, and Dr. Laura Hendrickson, *When Good Kids Make Bad Choices: Help and Hope for Hurting Parents* (Eugene, OR: Harvest House, 2005).

12. These include Prozac, Paxil, and Zoloft.

13. http://www.nlm.nih.gov/medlineplus/news/fullstory_29715.html.

14. Glenmullen, *Antidepressant Solution*, 70–71.

15. FDA Talk Paper T04-08, March 22, 2004. You can view this paper on the FDA website, www.fda.gov.

16. Glenmullen, *Prozac Backlash*, 30–48.

17. Healy, *Let Them Eat Prozac*, 112.

18. http://www.fda.gov/bbs/topics/NEWS/2005/NEW01270.html.

19. http://www.sciencedaily.com/releases/2006/02/060206232244.htm.

20. These include Klonopin, Ativan, and Xanax.

21. These include Ambien, Halcion, and Restoril.

22. Brand names include Eskalith and Lithobid.

23. These include Depakote, Tegretol, Lamictal, and Topamax.

24. These include Haldol and Prolixin.